PORTRAIT OF A
RAINBOW
AS A YOUNG MAN
AKA
Doberman's Angel

A Novel

Todd Crawshaw

CrowsnestPublishing.com

www.toddcrawshaw.com

ISBN-10: 1-7333502-0-9
ISBN-13: 978-1-7333502-0-4

Cover art and design by author

CrowsnestPublishing.com

Printed in the United States of America

END OF THE RAINBOW MEETS LIGHTNING IN A BOTTLE

"I have wanted to kill myself
a hundred times, but somehow
I am still in love with life."
— Voltaire, Candide

"When I went to school, they
asked me what I wanted to be
when I grew up. I wrote down
"Happy." They told me I didn't
understand the assignment,
and I told them they didn't
understand life."
— John Lennon

"How narrow is the vision
that exalts the busyness
of the ant above the singing
of the grasshopper."
— Khalil Gibran

"Be a rainbow
in someone else's cloud."
— Maya Angelou

1

Doberman hated Christmas. Bristol Sparks loved everything about it. The shiny ornaments and twinkling lights made her happy. The artificial displays declaring *joy-to-the-world* gave Doberman a headache. Snowflakes began to fall from the sky, prickling his skin. His mouth released a cloudy vapor as he cursed these icy particles. He tugged at the red woolen cap he had found on a bench. It barely covered his ears. His head was scrunched into his shoulders. When he happened to look up, the aberration of a little girl startled him. She was smiling, bundled in a white parka. Her green skirt matched her tights tucked into furry-white boots. Her long blond hair framed her face. A white pom-pom was attached to the tip of her green ski hat pulled down to her eyes.

Doberman was sitting on the cement and huddled against the doorway of a shuttered art gallery. The alcove partially sheltered him from the wind and kept him away from the sidewalk with its parade of holiday shoppers.

"Blanket?"

The girl held out the folded cloth in her arms.

"Go away," growled Doberman.

"You're cold."

"How would you know?"

"I'm cold too."

"Then *you* wear it."

She appeared to be alone, but he guessed the parents belonging to this do-gooder were hovering nearby, watching their little angel. He looked away, then up at her again. "Why are you here?"

"I'm Bristol Sparks."

He grunted a laugh. "Sounds about right. BS, to me."

"What's your name?"

He clenched his teeth and shivered. "*Do-ber-man.*"

"Oh, like the dog?"

He snarled, "Do I look like a dog?"

"I like your beard."

Reminded of its length, gone prematurely grey, now white, and flecked with ice particles, he said, "I'm *not* Santa Claus."

"I know that," she giggled.

A flurry of snowflakes stung his eyes and he ducked his head. "Maybe I was. Once. Long ago. Pretending to be Santa's little helper. Like you. Not anymore. Just ... Go away."

When Doberman looked up, the girl was gone.

The blanket lay at his feet.

2

Tober Chase was fourteen years old when struck by lightning. A rainbow appeared in the sky amidst a passing storm on Christmas morning. He had run outside to witness the arching spectral colors. The blast shredded his clothing and knocked him unconscious. He awoke to find his skin scarred with a permanent fractal pattern that trailed from his chest to his navel. The lightning strike had routed down the wires of his iPod, a present which he had unwrapped only hours before the incident. The emergency room doctor believed that this gift from his parents had diverted the 300,000 volts of electricity away from his heart and other vital organs and saved his life.

During his three-day hospital internment for observation, Tober had a mental reconstitution which he equated as being an epiphany. Whether (or not) this jolt of energy to his neurological system had somehow rewired his brain, he decided to interpret this electrostatic discharge to his body as a sign – that God had selected him to be a conduit for good and help make the world a better place.

As the holidays came to an end, Tober celebrated the new year by truncating his given name into one word: Chase. To his parents' chagrin, he discarded "Tober" because he said it represented a pupal stage of his metamorphosis, like a disposable chrysalis, thereby of no further use. He next sought to overcome his heretofore disposition of shyness and timidity. While riding on the school bus, he witnessed an older boy bullying a smaller kid and Chase stood up to stop it. For his courage, he was slugged in the face. The crack of cartilage and blood that gushed from his nose, he had not anticipated. Chase staggered backwards and fell into his seat. He realized God had not provided him with any super powers. He was vulnerable, left to rely on his own volition, and prone to error.

Kay Foster, a girl he barely knew, came to his aid to nurse him. She put her scarf to his face and instructed him to look up as she held his head. Once the blood coagulated and the bleeding had stopped, Chase was smitten by this girl, by her beautiful smile and kind eyes. She too was a sign, he intuited, and predicted she would become an integral part of his life.

—◦◦◦—

Chase decided to trust God and continue to be communicative. Previously, he had been afraid to voice his feelings. Settling into his desk for his first class of the day, he looked across the aisle at the boy who sat closest to him.

"Hi, I'm Chase."

"I know who you are."

"Not really. We've hardly ever talked."

"Because you're weird."

"Not by choice. Your name is Norman, right?"

The boy gave him a cold stare. "What's with your nose?"

Chase felt his nostrils. His nose was still sore, but hadn't begun to bleed again. "Someone hit me this morning."

"Were you really struck by lightning?"

"Yeah. Christmas morning."

"That's weird. What did it feel like?"

"It hurt. Really bad. I have a permanent scar now."

"What kind of scar?"

"Across my chest. It's called a fractal pattern."

"Cool. Let me see."

The teacher broke up their conversation by calling their names, asking them to solve algebra problems written on the blackboard.

"I'll show you after school."

"Okay. And don't *ever* call me Norman. It's Norm."

Word spread about this scar caused by lightning. After the last bell, kids assembled in the parking lot waiting for the big reveal.

Chase arrived and was approached by a boy named Derick who, along with Norm, belonged to a club with a reputation for partying and wild behavior. Derick, a junior, poked Chase in the chest.

"Let's see that scar."

Chase obliged, unzipping his jacket, then unbuttoning his shirt. He spread open both articles of clothing, exposing bare skin and the disfigurement. The reddish scar resembled a fern leaf instead of chest hairs that trailed from his neck to navel.

Derick smirked. "I always knew you were a freak."

This classification and snub bewildered Chase.

Derick laughed. "Look, Clark Kent thinks he's Superman."

He punctuated this remark with a sucker punch. Chase buckled over and dropped to his knees.

Norm said, "What the hell! Why did you do that, Derick?"

"I felt like it. What's it to you? Let's go."

Derick turned to leave.

As Chase caught his breath, he said, "If you keep doing that, you'll regret it someday."

Derick turned around. "What'd you say?"

Still on the ground, Chase said, "Your fear. It's misplaced."

Derick stormed back. Norm stood between them. "Come on, man. Leave him alone. He didn't do anything."

Derick pushed Norm and pointed at Chase, "Hey, loser, I'm not afraid of anyone. Especially not you! You got that?"

Chase stood, holding his stomach. "Loud and clear. *'There's nothing to fear but fear itself,'* said FDR."

"Who?"

"Forget it. I'm not your enemy, Derick."

That evening while seated at the dinner table with his parents, his mother asked Chase how his first day back to school went.

"Pretty good. I made two new friends.

3

Doberman was shuffling along the city sidewalk clutching the large blanket. He resembled a bedraggled king with his long white beard, red hat, and large blanket held around his neck like a cape. The long cloth brushed the ground behind him. Shakespeare's King Lear plagued his mind. For he felt like a tragic hero whose hubris had caused his downfall. With no clear destination in mind, he moved along, lost within the swarm of holiday shoppers, theater goers, and tourists, all of whom parted, like the Red Sea, clearing a path for him.

These sidewalk evening interlopers either stared or looked away. To some he was a pitiful creature, while to others invisible – at least, they pretended he was. It was hard to fathom, even for himself, how he had arrived at this point in time. This was not at all what he had imagined his life would become.

He paused to look up at the two-to-three story Christmas tree in the middle of Union Square. It was lit up with a swirl of colorful lights and gigantic glittering balls. Next came a skating rink created for the season, a flood of water frozen into ice so skaters could glide and twirl upon its surface. People were laughing and appeared to be happy, or at least content, moving in family units, some as couples walking hand-in-hand, many carrying packages, others dressed up in their finery for a festive dinner, or to attend the theater.

His eyes threatened to expose tears and Doberman clutched the blanket, swiping with the back of his hand to stifle this overt display of sorrow. At a peering toddler nearby, he grunted a *ho-ho-ho* and winked, then grimaced, as he hobbled down the few steps to reach street level. A clanging cable car crowded with passengers, several hanging from its sides, was being pulled uphill. He walked across the tracks, causing cars to honk.

About to turn and head up the block to find another alcove for the night, he spotted the little girl in the white parka, green skirt, tights, and matching hat. She was standing at the curb, waiting at the crosswalk. Doberman paused and noticed the signal light changing from a red hand to a white man walking. The girl, looking straight ahead and waving at someone, stepped off the curb – about to cross over to the other side.

The downtown noise was deafening, but Doberman heard then saw the automobile accelerate, racing through the red light. He ran and dove – shoving the girl out of the path of the car.

The impact was severe, sending Doberman airborne. He landed hard on the road. The shock and pain stunned him. Facing upward, he lay there, unable to move, but felt ice particles landing gently on his forehead. Amidst the discordant sounds of horns, shouts, and a choir singing Silent Night, he heard screaming from the girl, prior to his senses shutting down, plunging him into unconsciousness.

4

Chase saw Kay Foster through the school bus window. He watched as she disappeared and reappeared, rising up the stairs. Bundled in a blue rain coat and holding a backpack, she stopped at the empty seat beside him and sat down.

"How's your nose?" she said.

"Better," he said. "I don't think it's broken."

"Let me look." She gave his face a closer inspection. She softly pinched the bridge of his nose. "Does that hurt?"

"It actually feels kinda nice."

She withdrew her hand and questioned his smile.

"Thanks for yesterday," he said.

"My mother's a nurse. I guess I take after her."

"What does your father do?"

She looked down to unzip her backpack and rummage around for something inside. "A business man. He went away."

"Does he travel a lot?"

"You want to share this?" She held up a granola bar.

"Okay. Is that your breakfast?"

"Sometimes. What about your parents?"

9

"My dad works for the government. Social services. I'm not sure actually what he does."

"Do you like playing sports?"

"Not especially. Sort of. Why?"

"I don't know. Just asking. What does your mother do?"

"She's a child therapist. Why is that funny?"

Kay shook her head. "It's not. Sorry. I didn't mean to—"

"Other kids say things about me. I know that."

"My mother told me you were hit by lightning. She saw you at the hospital. She also said you're lucky to be alive."

"We all are. I think what happened to me was a sign."

"How do you mean?"

Chase took a bite of the granola bar, hesitant to speak openly and risk losing a friend, assuming she considered him to be one. He swallowed, before prefacing with, "You'll think it's weird."

"Maybe." Kay grinned. "What kind of sign?"

His shyness briefly returned. "I like talking to you."

"Same here. What kind of a sign?"

"From God. For me to start doing good things."

Kay ate the last piece of her granola. She crunched the wrapper into a ball and gave him a direct look. "I'd call that weird."

They both laughed.

"It is, you're right," he said.

"I know I am," she teased. "Wow, how bad do you have to be to have God zap you with a lightning bolt?"

"I wondered that too. The odds of getting struck by lightning is like one in a million."

"Less than that, actually."

"Was I randomly selected? Which sounds stupid. More like it was wrong place, wrong time. Just forget everything I said."

"No way. Let's say it's true. What's your plan?"

"I don't have one. I know it's changed me."

"How?"

"I'm not as shy. And I'm more optimistic."

"About?"

"The future. Like what we're going to become."

"What?"

"I don't know. Anything we want. We have to believe it."

"Okay, you first? What do you want to be?"

"I'm good with my hands. Working with wood."

"Wood?"

"Creating things. What about you?"

"I'll end up being a nurse, probably, like my mom."

"Why not a doctor?"

"Maybe."

"You've never dreamed of being anything else?"

"It'll sound stupid."

"No it won't."

"Designing homes. Interior spaces. I'd like doing that."

"Why?'

Kay zipped up her backpack and held it to her chest. "Because home is where you feel safe. A place to nourish your soul." She made a face and laughed. "*Gawd*, that does sound stupid. And weird."

"I don't think you're weird or stupid."

"Thanks." Kay stood as the bus pulled into the schoolyard. "I didn't lie about my dad. He did go away, not because he's a pilot or always traveling on business. He went away because he's an asshole. He yelled and hit my mom. I remember being afraid of him. That's all I remember. I was five when he left home."

Chase's world view was expanding. He had never ventured far from home. His travels amounted to a few trips to the city, a fifteen mile drive. For a vacation, his parents took him once to Disneyland. That was the extent of his exposure to other worlds. He now realized

11

there were many worlds to explore right in front of him. As the bus came to a stop, he said goodbye to Kay. They went separate ways. The courtyard was already teeming with student bodies assembled in its variety of groups defined by age, gender, and popularity.

Being struck by lightning caused Chase to see these groups as if they were foreign countries. He knew virtually nothing about these other kids. They were designated territories he had yet to experience. He would veer away, avoiding contact, moving between these cliques which projected vibes as palpable as force fields that repelled a stray electron. Once he had reached his locker in the hallway, he felt safe. Then inside the classrooms he felt protected wedged within his desk. He ate alone during lunchtime.

Today, he penetrated one of these exclusive magnetic fields to reach Norm who was standing with his friends. They were hovered loosely near the fountain before the first morning bell.

"Hey," he said.

Norm turned and appeared surprised to see him standing there. "Hey, sorry about yesterday. Derick can be a Dick."

"That's okay. I've been hit harder."

Norm grinned. "By lightning. You're a legend."

Chase shrugged. "I don't think his anger was really meant for me anyway."

"Once you get to know him, he's not such a bad guy."

"If you say." Chase turned to go. "See you in class."

"Later. Hey. That's an awesome scar."

5

Voice recognition. It was heard within the depths of a dream as he entered semi-consciousness. His head was throbbing. The side of his body, leg, and ankle, ached too. The pain was overwhelming. He lay immobile on a warm bed of cement. He was detecting a clean, antiseptic smell.

The voice came again. "That's the name he told me."

"Doberman. You're sure?"

"Pretty sure. Yes, I'm very sure."

"He has no identification. We labeled him a John Doe."

"Will he be okay?"

It was the girl's voice again. Doberman knew her. Someone from his childhood. He struggled to remember who.

"How bad was he injured?" It was a man's voice.

"He had a concussion. It's uncertain whether there will be any permanent damage. He suffered five broken ribs. A punctured lung. Broken leg and a fractured ankle. He's lucky to be alive."

Lucky to be alive.

The words came from a women. They seemed to float then fade. His eyes opened. He was adjusting to the sharp lights.

"Look, he's awake!"

Doberman saw the elf, then recognized the girl from the street. Her excited smile was comforting.

"Where am I?"

Several other people were there. One was a doctor, identifiable by her green surgery scrubs and stethoscope.

"You're a lucky man," she told him.

"Why am I here?"

"A car hit you," she said.

"You saved my life," said the girl.

The doctor asked, "How much do you remember?"

"Bits and pieces." Doberman scanned the room and determined he was in an ICU room. His arm was attached to an IV. There was also beeping equipment monitoring his body.

"You had no identification on you. What's your name?"

"Doberman."

"I told you," said the girl.

A man put his hand on her shoulder. The father, he guessed.

"Is that your last name?" asked the doctor.

"It's my only name." Doberman saw two other men standing at the foot of the hospital bed. One was a police officer.

The other one spoke, saying, "Mr Doberman—"

"It's just Doberman."

The man went on to say, "One of the emergency room doctors recognized you. From having visited us before. This is now the third time you've tried to kill yourself."

"How dare you! This man saved my daughter's life."

"Mr. Sparks, I appreciate your view. But I was notified by other physicians. And I've studied this man's record."

"Who are you?"

"I'm Doctor Stevens. I oversee the psychiatric unit"

"Excuse me, Doctor," said the father. "This wasn't an attempted suicide. It was an act of heroics."

"Mr. Sparks, this man lives on the streets. He's homeless. And our records clearly indicate there is a pattern—"

"To hell with your records! I'm a retired army sergeant. I know bravery when I see it. I was on the opposite side of the street, waiting for my daughter to cross, when a speeding car ran the red light and nearly killed her. And he *would* have had this man *not* pushed her out of the way, sacrificing himself."

"Nevertheless, because—"

"What do you plan to do with him?"

Existentially fascinated, Doberman observed this back and forth discussion about his fate and state of existence.

"Since he is homeless, has no means of support, or the ability to pay for his healthcare – which we, the taxpayers, are obliged by state law to provide free of charge – and given his history of emergency care, I have the authority to hold and commit him to the department of psychiatric care for evaluation. Either that, or we send him back into the streets. Do you have a better plan?"

"We could take him in," said the girl.

"Bristol," said the father. "That's not something—"

"He could stay in our guest house. Where grandma was before she died. It's empty now."

"Sweetie."

"Not advisable," Stevens chimed in. "Really, it's not—"

"Dad, until he gets better."

"We don't ... Excuse us, Doberman. We—"

Doberman waved a dismissive hand. "Not a problem."

"Bristol, the doctors here know—"

"He saved my life!"

The father was in a quandary of emotions, painfully conflicted, wanting to do the right thing in the presence of his daughter.

The woman doctor was curiously taking it all in too, remaining neutral, until she surprised them all. "From what I've been told by my colleagues, who have treated this man before, he's shown to have a good heart, and has never exhibited violent behavior."

"He needs our help, Daddy. Please?"

"As an incentive," added the woman, "If you were to seriously consider this temporary housing situation, I'd be more than willing to make house visits, as his physician, until he recovers fully."

"Seriously, Dr. Evans? What you're proposing is—"

"Please?" Bristol pleaded. "He needs a home."

"Hey, BS," hissed Doberman. "Remember, I'm not a dog."

6

Chase stopped in the hallway by the auditorium to peruse the bulletin board. The prominent flyer had dayglow images depicting a golden brick road winding toward a distant glittering emerald city. Posted by the Drama Department, it announced the Spring musical: Wizard of Oz. There was a sign-up sheet for any student wanting to audition. He looked closer to see if he recognized any of the names. As a freshman, he knew hardly any upperclass students, except for a few notable standouts who always made sure they were known. One name on the list of entries stood out: Kay Foster.

He determined the flyer to be another sign. Grabbing the pencil dangling from a string held by a pushpin stuck into the corkboard, he wrote his name on the list. Perplexed by what it all meant, since he had no experience performing on a stage or ever singing in public, Chase knew enough to know he needed to act. So he signed up. He re-read the print to make sure there were no requirements stating the participants needed to be students enrolled in a drama class.

A week later, he was among the other wannabe actors in the auditorium to receive printed handouts of the script to take home and read before returning the next week for auditions. During the commotion of the first assembled reading, the teacher, a Ms. Havish, who would be directing this production, made it known she was a graduate of Juilliard in New York City and recited her achievements on Broadway and in Hollywood. Therefore, to make this enterprise worthy of her ample talent and precious time, she would require their adolescent undivided attention, respect, and devotion.

Chase was left wondering what career calamity had occurred to cause Ms. Havish's demotion, employed here to instruct high-school students. Her time-consuming lecture negated an opportunity to talk with Kay, who waved and greeted him with a smile, then departed promptly when the cattle call ended.

Chase chose to read for the part of the Lion, whose character flaw was described as being one who lacked courage. He felt his pre-lightning pre-teen years of cowardice was a gold mine he could draw for inspiration. Despite his best efforts, he wasn't given the part. Nor did he receive a minor role as one of the singing munchkins, flying monkeys, or dancing poppies. Kay edged out others to be chosen understudy for the lead role of Dorothy, a major accomplishment, since she was a freshman. The lead went to a senior. Chase tried to cheer Kay up by effusively congratulating her.

"Hurrah for me," she quipped sourly. "I'll be standing behind the curtain. Never to be seen. Invisible. *Woopee.*"

"You were great. She gave me nothing. And I don't care."

"No—*wait!*" she voiced aloud. "What about Toto?"

"Excuse me?" said Ms. Havish, annoyed by the interruption.

"Chase could be Toto."

"There is no relevant part written for Toto in this script."

"Dorothy needs a Toto. No lines are required."

"I could play a dog," said Chase.

"You'd only get in the way," said the director.

Kay continued to insist there be a role for Toto. Because of her unrelenting advocacy on his behalf, Chase believed the subsequent ire and harsh treatment that Kay received was the reason. Once she'd broken the teacher's resolve – getting her to howl, *"Fine!* He can be Toto!" – Kay encountered overbearing criticism from Ms. Havish. Rehearsals came to a halt as Kay was berated before the entire cast for the way she delivered a line or sang a verse. It escalated until Ms. Havish achieved victory by tormenting Kay to the point of complete humiliation, causing her to run off in tears and threaten to quit.

Chase tried his best to console Kay by encouraging her to ignore the teacher's petty vindictiveness. "Her remarks are unjust, and not even related to your talent," he told her. "She knows you're talented and feels threatened. You challenged her in front of the class. She wants to belittle you to show everyone that she is the one in control. It's *her* problem, not yours."

Kay laughed and hugged Chase. They proceeded to join forces. They met after school and located on the internet a white one-piece pajama suit that, once delivered, they applied dark spots and painted paws on the feet. From a costume shop they purchased dog ears and face makeup to smear his face white before adding black patches.

Kay steadfastly remained positive during rehearsals despite the repetitive slights she received, disguised as constructive input from Ms. Havish. By now, Kay had accepted the fact she was being cast aside. Her resolve was to be cheerful despite it all and watch from the wings of the stage. Until opening night, when the lead Dorothy, plagued by a panic attack, broke out in hives and refused to perform. Horrified by this turn of events, Ms. Havish lashed out, irrationally shouting and expressing betrayal before reacting in a hair-pulling peevish reluctance – yet conceding there were no other viable options available – to hastily undress and redress (figuratively and literally) Kay as Dorothy and thrust her onto the stage as the lead.

Chase was in awe of Kay, trailing after her as her faithful dog throughout the show. At the reception which followed in the theater foyer, a congestion of attendees, comprising mostly of parents and friends, gathered to greet the cast. Kay was handed the bouquet of roses initially intended for the other Dorothy and she professed her appreciation. Among the many well-wishers was a reporter from the local newspaper and, while complimenting the entire production, lavished his praise on Kay's stellar performance. Standing next to her was Ms. Havish who directed her frozen smile at the reporter.

"Ms. Havish deserves the credit for pushing us all so very hard, those in front and behind the stage, to bring out our full potential. Theater is about everyone. It's really a collaborative effort."

Kay's unexpected and gracious compliment produced from Ms. Havish an uncharacteristic emotional outburst of tears.

Chase had been watching nearby and listening, standing alone in his dog suit. A woman approached him.

She said, "My daughter wants to meet you."

Chase looked down and saw a shy little girl looking up.

"You were my favorite," she told him.

Her eyes were wide with an adorable look of admiration.

His heart melted. "Thank you."

Chase had no ambition or illusion of ever being a professional actor, yet, at that moment, he realized any future accomplishments or acclaim he'd receive would never top this girl's star-struck smile.

7

Still absorbing the shock of this suspended-reality fast-transfer, Doberman peered around at the cozy room he had been transported into, after being rolled up a convenient ramp by wheelchair and set within the queen-size bed. It had been more than a year since he felt a mattress beneath his body instead of dirt or cement, not counting his two or three overnight hospital stays.

After the initial commotion of getting him moved and settled in, his caretakers encouraged him to get rest, then they left him alone. Upon the day of his arrival, which followed a trip across the bay, he had ample time to assess his present accommodations. He surmised the dwelling had once been a storage shed converted and remodeled. The two-room cottage, which included a bathroom, was situated on a wooded property featuring a patio area and garden separating this smaller dwelling from the main house.

He was watching a beam of sunlight that had entered through a window and was slowly crossing the room. There was a tapping on the door which faced his bed.

"Come in." He was confused by the passage of time.

Bristol Sparks stood in the open doorway. She held a small tray of food. "Are you hungry?"

"What time is it?"

"Almost eight." She stepped inside. "Did you sleep okay?"

"Never better." Doberman gave a terse smile, belatedly realizing he had slept through an entire night. He sat up in the bed, propping himself against the pillows and headboard. Sharp stabs of pain shot up to his brain from his ribs, leg and ankle. He winced.

"Are you okay?"

"I'll live. How are you doing?"

"Me? Are you kidding? You saved my freak'n life."

"It was nothing. Is that bacon?"

"And eggs. Are you a vegetarian?"

"I'm strickly vegan."

"Oh."

"I'm kidding. That's all for me?"

Bristol handed Doberman the bed tray and helped position it across his legs.

"Are you my nurse?"

"Sorta." She took a step back. "My dad said since I insisted on *adopting* you, his words, you've become my responsibility."

"What does your mother have to say about all this?"

Bristol turned away. "I need to go. Or I'll miss my bus and be late for school." She paused at the door. "My dad arranged to bring someone in to help. In case you need something. She stays overnight with me when my dad is away."

"A babysitter?"

"She's okay. I'll come visit you after school."

"Thank you," said Doberman.

"You're welcome."

As Bristol turned to leave, he said, "Hey."

She turned back. "What?"

"Woof."

After his breakfast, Doberman had nodded off into sleep again. When he opened his eyes there was a silhouetted figure standing in the doorway blocking the sun.

"Hello?"

"Yes, hello," said a woman's voice. She stepped inside the room. As she moved to the side of the bed, her facial features took form. She was middle-aged, attractive, with sharp features and suspicious squinting eyes. "You are homeless man?"

"I was. Am."

"Hum. Little Bristol, you save her, yes?"

"I suppose I did."

"You are good man."

"I think the jury is still out on that one."

"What jury?"

"Nothing. It's a figure of speech."

"My name Daleka. I too was homeless. In Slovakia. Both father, then mother die. Have older brother. We beg on streets. But survive. Gypsies take pity. They feed us. When older, they sell us."

"You were sold?"

"Sent to America. Work for bad man. Many men. Many years. But I escape. Brother not so lucky."

"I'm sorry."

"Yes, me too. Not like Mr. Sparks. He is good man."

Doberman was trying to follow her fragmented history.

"Mr. Sparks, he help me find work. Not bad work. Good work. Watching little Bristol. Now you. What is your story?"

"I don't like talking about it."

"Your story is bad too?"

"What did you say your name was again?"

"Daleka. And yours?"

"Doberman."

"Ah, yes, Bristol say. Like the dog."

"Don't worry," he quipped, "I *am* house trained."

"How d'you mean?"

"It was a joke."

"I no understand joke. Would you like lunch? I make you ham sandwich, yes?"

"I would love that."

"Okay. You are good man. Save Bristol. I be right back."

"You'll find me here. Or doing laps in the swimming pool."

Daleka paused to study his expression, looked at the wheelchair, his leg in a cast, his supine body. "No pool. This is joke, yes?"

"Is that a smile?"

Daleka blinked, her features darkening, turning red, before her face sharpened again. "I go make lunch. You stay."

8

Monday morning, following the three-day musical production of The Wizard of Oz, Chase looked for Kay but he didn't see her enter the bus. At her street-corner stop, the usual group of kids was standing there waiting, then clambered aboard, and took random seats. The bus drove off and Chase began to worry and wonder if Kay had become sick. He was eager to tell her again how great she was as Dorothy. Also to thank her for her part in landing him a role in the play as Toto. It had been fun pretending to be her dog.

Ms. Havish had been conflicted regarding what to do following Kay's surprise performance on opening night, which not only saved the play but won Ms. Havish acclaim, credited for the phenomenal production in reviews by the local newspapers. Thus, Ms. Havish's chilly opinion of Kay had warmed considerably and had altered her decision to reinstate the senior into the lead. Even after her once-favored-student cried and begged forgiveness, indicated her hives and nerves were gone. She resorted to screaming. Depriving her the role would ruin her chances of acceptance into top college theatrical programs. She threatened to recruit her parents to apply political and financial pressure (which she did) – but failed to sway Ms.

Havish. Kay kept the role of Dorothy.

With all this attention, Kay was suddenly launched from being a virtual unknown into the known. Thereby catching the eye of a junior student and star athlete who approached her after the Sunday matinee to ask if she would like a ride to school Monday morning. She accepted.

Once Chase had discovered this turn of events, he was puzzled and heartbroken. Was this part of God's plan? When he had seen Kay Foster's name on the audition sheet, he understood it to be a *sign* – to sign up and act! So he did, but had anticipated a completely different outcome. God spoke in mysterious ways, his mother had told him once, so Chase held firm to his lightning-strike epiphany, believing there must be a good reason why things unfolded the way they did.

"Hey, Toto!"

Chase acknowledged these occasional shout-outs with a smile, whether they were intended to be good-natured teasing or ridicule. He had become more recognizable, yet his newfound notoriety was not on the same scale as Kay's popularity. Chase would occasionally see her on the school campus as she was eating lunch with others, or passing in the hallways. They would exchange smiles, or stop for a curtailed talk, then go their separate ways.

Even though the outcome was not what Chase had hoped for – a closer relationship with Kay – his decision to take a chance and experience the theater had gained him respect among his peers. At least by some. And his confidence had grown. He now regularly entered the morning gatherings which took place by the fountain.

"How does it feel being a dog?" quipped Norm.

"Different," said Chase.

Derick viewed his presence among their tribe as an intrusion and asked him pointedly, "Meaning what, Toto?"

Chase grinned. "It gave me a new perspective on the world."

"Yeah, down on all fours. Is that how Kay likes it?"

The remark was barbed as a taunt with its sexual implication. Chase let it go with a smile while the others laughed.

The morning bell sounded and their huddle began to disperse. As it did, Derick challenged Chase. "Hey, Toto. Acting on stage is for pussies. Try out for football next year if you want to become a man instead of a dog!"

Chase shouted back, "Thanks. I'll consider it."

<hr />

Freshman year ended uneventfully with Chase receiving passing grades without much effort. He scored the occasional A and C, but mostly he was a B student. Encouraged by Norm, he had signed up to compete in Spring track. When he failed to do well at throwing a shot put, javelin, discus, hammer, or leaping in the long jump, high jump, and pole vault, he opted for cross country. He could run. Not fast, but far. During these distance treks he had time to think about his life and determined God was sending him another message.

Chase asked his parents for money with a promise to pay them back. With the loan, he purchased a set of dumbbells, an adjustable workout bench, and a pull-up bar apparatus which he attached to a doorway in their garage. To build up his leg muscles and endurance, he ran a mile each morning holding two ten-pound rocks.

Chase worked the summer months as a waiter at the local pizza parlor. Amidst the interminable clatter and repetitive order taking, he found he liked talking to people. Except when Kay appeared on dates with her boyfriend Jake, a junior who wasn't going away but returning next year as a senior. Chase would deliver their food with feigned alacrity, presenting a convivial smile. Even though it hurt to see Kay attached with someone else.

A few weeks before school commenced, Chase received what he believed to be a new *sign*. Derick appeared with a cadre of his unruly friends. Students from another school, who belonged to a rival club, were eating pizza at another table. Words were exchanged between the two groups, which escalated to insults with Derick being shoved. A fight broke out.

Chase had been instructed, as part of his job description, to call the police or intercede when there was trouble. Fortunately, one of the waiters was an experienced bouncer having worked at nightclubs and promptly helped break up the brawl.

Unfazed by his expulsion, Derick was laughing insouciantly and noticed Chase. "Hey, Toto. Hell Week coming fast. Sign up. Become a jock, man, if you ever want to attract the chicks!"

9

As Doberman awoke, he saw a miniature Christmas tree on the bookshelf beside the front door. It was aglow with twinkling lights. The windows of his cottage room were black, indicating it was night. He sat up in bed. The pain from his leg and ribs was throbbing. He saw a glass of water on a table beside the bed. He removed two more capsules the pharmacy had provided to lessen the pain, swallowing them in one gulp. He stroked his beard and peered around the dark interior. The silence was disquieting. It was the absence of noise. There were no sounds of passing cars or police sirens. He heard a faint rhymic chirping. Then a knocking.

"Come in."

The door opened. Bristol Sparks came into view holding a tray. "You slept through dinner. So I came to see if you were awake. Are you hungry?"

"What's that sound?"

Bristol paused to listen, then smiled. "Crickets."

"Crickets?"

"You've never heard crickets before?"

"Of course I have." He pointed at the small tree decorated with its swirl of colorful lights. "Is that your doing?"

"Pretty, isn't it?"

"What's for dinner?"

"A chicken pasta. Daleka made it."

"She's here?"

"She left. My dad's home."

Bristol came forward and handed him the tray. He positioned it on the bed over his body.

"How was school today?"

"Okay. Until Billy Owens pulled my hair and pinched me."

"Who's Billy?"

"He's on your naughty list."

Doberman chuckled. "I'll check. Maybe he likes you."

"No. He got sent to the principal's office."

"Boys are weird."

"No kidding. What about you?"

"What about me?"

"You were a boy. Once."

Doberman picked up the fork and twirled the pasta and brought it to his mouth. "Santa was never a boy."

"So now you're saying you *are* him."

"A figment of your imagination? Sure, why not?"

Bristol folded her arms. "You think I'm gullible. A stupid kid. I'm ten. I don't believe in fairy tales."

"Me neither. This pasta is really good."

"I'm glad you saved my life. But what's your story. Why were you living and sleeping on the streets?"

He pointed to the pasta. "Delicious."

"Daleka couldn't get anything from you either. Why?"

"Why does it matter?"

"Because you're living in our guest house."

"Not by choice. Remember, it was *you* who adopted me."

"My father wants to speak with you."

"About?"

"You can ask him yourself. He'll be here soon. You're always asleep when he comes over. You sleep a lot."

"It's been a tough year."

"Is that how long you've been homeless?"

"Could be two. I've lost count."

"What happened to you?"

Doberman wiped his mouth with a napkin. "Life."

———

Sparks was standing outside and listening. The door had been left ajar. He stepped inside. His grey business suit complemented his slender frame. The collar of his white shirt was unbuttoned and his gold necktie pulled loose.

"Good evening."

Doberman nodded. "Good evening to you, Mr. Sparks."

"Call me David."

"David."

"And you, it's just Doberman? No first name?"

"It would only get in the way."

Sparks smiled, accepting the remark as a joke. He turned to his daughter. "Sweetie, give us some time alone. And feed Mozart."

"Who's Mozart?" said Doberman.

"A very famous composer. *Duh*," said Bristol.

"He's our dog," said Sparks.

"Wolfgang. We call him that too. He's an Afghan Hound."

"Bristol, now? And close the door behind you, please."

"I'll see you later, Doberman."

Bristol departed with a playful wave and meandered from the cottage. Once outside, she ever-so-slowly shut the door.

Sparks raised his eyebrows at Doberman. "My daughter."

"I like her."

31

"Me too."

"Is Bristol your only child?" As Doberman sat up higher against the headboard, Sparks pulled a chair toward the bed and sat.

"Let's talk about you first. I took you in."

"And I'm grateful."

"It was at Bristol's insistence. Not knowing much if anything about you. I agreed, well, because you saved her life."

"Which I would do again."

"She's all I have. To answer your question. Her mother, my wife, and her brother were killed by a drunk driver five years ago."

"I'm sorry. That's horrible."

"Yes, it was. And is. Still. What about you, Doberman?"

"What about me?"

"I did some investigating, just so you know. I wasn't about to take in a stranger to stay in our guest cottage, at least without some knowledge about the person. I checked with the police. They have no record or files on you. You've never been arrested?"

"Never."

"You're basically an unknown. Except for the doctors who said they've treated you before. And folks at the soup kitchens."

"I dislike that term."

"You know what I mean. Shelters. Anyway, those who've made contact with you. They vouch that you're a non-violent person."

"Good to hear. I would like to think I am."

"What caused you to be living on the streets?"

"I have no home."

"Yes, of course. But why? What are your circumstances?"

Doberman stroked his beard, pursing his lips tightly.

"Have you ever been married?"

"Once."

"Children?"

"Yes."

"What happened?"

"It didn't work out."

"What didn't?"

"Life."

"Meaning?"

"Death."

Sparks patiently waited for more to come from Doberman who, after more rubs to his lips and beard, spoke haltingly.

"It happens, David. As you well know. You don't ever expect it. But it does come. And it's personal. So I'd rather not talk about this. Though I do appreciate your hospitality. And your lovely daughter, who I'd gladly save again, if need be. But, please, respect my wishes. You see, I don't really know anything about you either. Except that you've graciously arranged for me to be transported into your house, and life, so to speak. You can throw me out if you want. I honestly don't care anymore. I'm unable to bare my soul to you. Not now. Maybe never. Okay?"

Sparks pushed back his chair and stood. "Okay."

"Thank you."

"Another time, maybe. Good night, Doberman."

10

Hell Week was called hell for good reason. After signing up for football, receiving a doctor's medical approval to play, acquiring a mouth guard from his dentist, his parents authorizing the decision by signing waivers and all required forms, Chase showed up at the boy's school locker room to be measured and sized for his protective gear. Equipped with the requisite accoutrements of helmet, shoulder pads, stretch pants with built-in cushions for knees, hip, thigh, then issued a jersey, he was nearly ready to participate. Cleated shoes, jockstrap and cup were the last items, purchased at a store.

Chase wore the number 27.

The grueling pre-school, week-long, two-times-a-day, morning and afternoon, practices began at 6:00 am sharp. All players were to be outfitted in their armor and on the football field. The coaches instructed them to do stretching warm-ups, including jumping jacks and sit-ups upon the dewy field. The remnant scent of wet mowed grass would haunt Chase's olfactory memory for years. Though he hated every second, getting wet and chilled before his body warmed by the rising sun to become overheated and then sweating profusely, he was determined to endure the abuse and make the team.

He tackled dummies, ran drills, and learned scrimmage plays. At a midday water break, he noticed several girls wearing matching skirts bouncing around at the opposite end of the field. He wandered over with Norm and a couple other players to see what was going on. Kay Foster was among the group. They were trying out for the cheerleading squad. Chase removed his helmet and waved. Kay saw him, appeared surprised and grinned, giving him an enthusiastic wave back.

"Hey, Dude. That's Conner's girl. Careful."

"Of what?" said Chase. "It's not like she's his property."

"Tell that to Jake," said Norm.

Chase shrugged and shook his head. "I doubt Kay realizes she's become an acquisition."

One of their coaches was yelling from downfield for them to get their asses back into practice.

"Yeah," laughed Norm. "Like we haven't become acquisitions. We'd better hustle or he'll make us run The Hill."

As they ran, recapping their heads with helmets and attaching chin straps, Chase said to Norm, "I knew there was a good reason why I signed up to play football. That there was a sign."

"What do you mean, a sign?"

"Forget it. You wouldn't understand."

"Understand what?"

"I'm not sure I understand either. Not yet anyway."

"Hey, Chase?"

"Yeah?"

Norm laughed, "You *are* weird."

—◦◦◦—

After football practices, the boy's gym was loud and boisterous. Cleats clacking against cement walkways, equipment getting shoved into metal lockers, doors slamming shut, along with towel swiping, shouts and laughter. Within the communal shower stalls with spouts of steaming water sprayed from the walls, there would be the overt and covert body inspections and comparisons regarding each other's masculinity. The hot water would aggravate Chase's fractal scar that trailed from his chest to his navel, turning it red, which became a source of fascination and target of verbal exchanges.

"Chase, you were damned lucky," shouted Derick between spits of water, "If your iPod had hung any lower, that bolt of lightning would've turned your weenie into a roast."

As Chase laughed with the others, he noticed the faint scars on Derick's back. Also a red welt on his hip. "That's one nasty bruise. Did you get that during practice today?"

Derick walked away, ignoring his question, grabbing his towel off a hook.

Chase was later seated next to Norm on a bench. As they were getting dressed in their street clothes, he asked in a whisper, "What's with Derick? All those scars on his back?"

Norm glanced around before saying, "When he was a kid, his dad used to whip him with a belt. As punishment."

"That's child abuse."

"Try telling that to his father. And I never told you anything about this. Alright?"

"Yeah, sure."

11

Doberman woke to a soft yet persistent knocking. He realized from the defused light on the window shades it was early morning. The door opened a crack.

"May I come in?"

Doberman recognized the woman. She was the emergency room doctor who had treated him at the hospital.

"I was on my way into the city. I wanted to stop by to check on you. Mr. Sparks told me I'd find you here."

"And here I am. Make yourself at home."

Dr. Evans was carrying a medical bag. She removed her overcoat and was wearing a red dress. Her green hospital scrubs had made her seem drab. While giving the room a quick inspection, she noticed the small Christmas tree and smiled. She moved her attention onto other items, the wheelchair, the crutches, then back to Doberman.

"How's your leg?"

"Itches."

"That's normal. You'll have the cast for a few more weeks." She came to the bed. "Your ribs?"

"They hurt. Slightly less."

"About six weeks for those to heal, too. I brought you more pills for the pain. Nothing addictive."

"Good to know. Wouldn't want to get hooked."

"Have you ever had a drug problem?"

"No."

"Any alcohol abuse issues?"

"I like a fine wine. A couple years since I've had a glass."

"Let me take a look at the head injury." She felt the skin beneath his hair. "Swelling has subsided. Any noticeable repercussions?"

"I'm sorry, who are you again?"

"I'm Dr. Evans. I was the emergency—"

"I'm joking. My mind is working fine. It does still hurt. But not as bad. The concussion actually helped clear my head."

She smiled, not sure whether to laugh or scowl. Was he joking, or showing signs of traumatic brain injury? Her creased forehead indicated a stalemate. "Can you get to the bathroom all right?"

"I manage. I've dealt with worse situations."

"Any questions for me?"

"Yes. Why are you doing this?"

"It's my profession."

"A doctor who makes house calls?"

"Not ordinarily."

"Why me?"

"That is a good question."

"I thought so. Have a seat. Stay awhile."

"I need to leave. I wanted to make sure you were okay."

"Better than okay. Do you have a less formal name?"

"Evie. Friends call me that. Is it still only Doberman?"

"Yes. It's strange, Evie. I feel like we've met before."

"In the emergency room."

"Somewhere else."

"A head injury coupled with sedatives can do that. It's not that uncommon. I should be going, or I'll be late for work."

"One favor. The door, leave it open. I like the fresh air."

"It's a beautiful day. Use the wheelchair or crutches to get out of bed and experience it yourself."

"I might consider it."

"I'll come back to check on you before Christmas."

"That's not necessary."

"I promised the Sparks that I would. And I want to."

Doberman struggled to get out of the bed and to the bathroom. Navigating his broken leg in its cast was problematic. Each shift of his body reverberated pain like a broken xylophone from his ribs. He planted his right foot on the floor, then pulled his plastered leg across the bed, holding it with both hands and setting it down. He lifted himself upright with the aid of his crutches and lumbered into the bathroom where there was a raised toilet seat with safety bars. These bars and handles were installed throughout the cottage. He recalled Bristol mentioning her grandmother had lived here.

The round trip from bed to bathroom took Doberman several minutes to complete. Once situated back in the bed, he sighed from the effort and closed his eyes. When he reopened them, he saw a large dark, long-haired dog sitting on the floor by the open doorway. Its head was poised, looking regal, staring at him.

"Mozart, I presume?"

The dog eagerly wagged its tail.

Bristol appeared holding a tray of food.

"Is it my feeding time again?"

"Mozart has already been fed. Afghan meet Doberman."

"Favoritism, I can abide. He looks likable."

Mozart came over to sniff and lick his fingers. Bristol nudged the dog aside to set the tray on the bed.

"He likes you."

"What time is it?"

"8:30."

"Didn't you miss the school bus?"

"We're on Christmas break."

"Ah," said Doberman. "I forgot. Santa's coming to town."

"I know, so much to do in just one night. You'll be needing all your strength."

Doberman smiled and tasted the scrambled eggs.

Bristol said, "Would you like me to entertain you?"

"What did you have in mind?"

"Eat first. I'll be back in a few minutes. And don't feed Mozart your bacon. It's not good for him."

"But it's okay for me? You're playing favorites again."

Mozart turned tail, following Bristol out the door.

<hr />

Bristol reappeared holding a violin and bow.

Doberman, while wiping his mouth and beard with the napkin, perked up with interest. "What's this?"

"It's called a violin, Doberman. A musical instrument."

"Which evolved during the Renaissance from its more common ancestor, the medieval fiddle. The modern violin is probably the best known and most widely distributed musical instrument in the world. Are you going to play something for me?"

"That was the idea. Be kind, I'm still learning."

"Aren't we all."

Bristol pulled forward a stool and sat, positioning the violin under her chin. She lifted the bow. "Ready?"

"Amaze me."

"See if you recognize the music."

Doberman listened to the sour vibrations of horsehairs scraping over steel strings, but was able to recognize the opening notes to one of Mozart's famous serenades. Holding a smile, he closed his eyes and waited for the torturous sounds to cease. When they did, after an elongated minute, he opened his eyes.

"Now that. Was simply. Horrible."

Bristol burst into laughter.

Doberman realized the joke and laughed with her.

"I wanted to see if you'd be honest with me."

"*Eine Kleine Nachtmusik.* The German title, which translates to *A Little Night Music.* Serenade No. 13 in G Major. A piece admired for its lively, joyful melody. Discounting your rendition."

"How did you know that?"

Doberman held out his hand. "May I try?"

Bristol stood and handed him the violin and bow.

As she took away his bed tray, setting it on a table, he plucked the strings. "Sounds to be in tune." He tucked back his long beard and placed his jaw on the chinrest. He raised the bow and played the same opening notes of the Mozart serenade, but with perfect clarity and precision.

Bristol's mouth opened wide. "How did you *do* that?"

"Santa knows a few tricks." He winked and handed her back the instrument.

"You're freaking me out. A little."

"No need. I took a music course in high school. I was horrible at learning how to read music. I nearly flunked the class. But I was determined to perfect and play one song on one instrument. And this happened to be the instrument and piece of music I chose."

"Still, a little freaky. I'm not as bad as what you heard before, but not good either. Will you teach me how to play like that?"

"It would be my pleasure. Mozart *is* the only piece I know. Your dream, is it to be a concert violinist?"

"No. Not really."

"Then what *is* your dream?"

"I love to draw and paint. To be an artist."

"Admirable. A world without art would be sad and lonely, like a string quartet without violins."

"My teacher said art is superfluous, whatever that means."

"Non essential. And no *real* teacher would say that."

"Then you'll be my teacher?"

"I can't draw or paint to save my life. But I am willing to teach you what I know about the violin. Music too has colors."

"No it doesn't."

Doberman gave her a spirited frown. "Once you learn to listen and hear the notes clearly, then you will see the rainbow."

12

At the end of Hell Week, Chase was notified by the coaches he had not made the varsity team. He would play for the junior varsity. New to tackle football, Chase didn't mind. But Norm, as a junior, groused repeatedly. Both were assigned to be halfbacks. At the end of each game, win or lose, Chase felt he had accomplished a victory. The camaraderie and collaborative effort was similar to what he had experienced participating in the making of a theatrical production. He enjoyed being part of a team.

At scrimmages, Chase excelled at homing in on the ball carrier and tackling the target on downfield runs. This won him a coveted spot on the kickoff squad. "Suit up and take the field!" That was the rally cry from their coaches before games to galvanize and coalesce their rabble energy into focus. Chase got nervous before each game, which hijacked his body into fits of yawning. Before a kickoff he would run in place to shake off his nerves and clear his thoughts. As their team aligned on one side of the field, facing their opposition, the padded armor and jerseys they wore to identify who was who, friend or foe, conjured images in Chase's mind of warriors bearing tribal banners and preparing for battle.

Once the ball was kicked, culminating in a collision of blocks and tackles, his insecurities and anxiety vanished. But whenever he was placed on the bench for too long, Chase would lose focus. The coaches picked up on this inherent flaw so, to keep him as an asset, they worked him to exhaustion, which kept him focused.

The Friday night varsity games were considered the pinnacle for expressing school spirit and pride. Both he and Norm would attend, sitting with their respective dates. From the bleachers, Chase would look down on Kay who was one of the chosen cheerleaders. She was unavoidably distracting, prominently situated between field and his line of vision during games. Their choreographed jumps and shouts only made Chase ache with unrequited love. He cheered with the rest, yet harbored jealously. Kay's boyfriend Jake, a wide receiver, often scored the touchdowns, and Chase suspected her cheers were more for him than their team. Derick, who Chase was still trying to figure out, played both offensive and defensive tackle and brutalized the opposing school.

Between classes, Chase stopped to sit on a courtyard bench to sort through notes for his next class. Someone sat beside him.

"What has God been telling you? Any new *signs?*"

"Oh." Chase was surprised to see Kay. "Hi."

She grinned. "I didn't mean to sound sarcastic."

Chase laughed. "I think you did."

"Maybe. A little. Have you?"

"God's been giving me the silent treatment."

"Grease. The Spring musical. *Sign* up sheet. It's been posted."

"I don't think so. Not this year."

"Football. So, what next? I watched a few of your home games. With my friend Jules. FYI – She likes you."

"Julia Winston? I had no idea."

"Chase, you need to focus and be more aware."

46

Her words made him smile. "I've missed talking with you."

"Ask her out. We can double date."

"Jules. Hum. She *is* kinda cute."

"No, *puppies* are cute. Jules is pretty."

"Not as pretty as you."

Kay frowned to show a playful yet curious scornful disapproval before standing and looked down at him. "Call her."

"*Okay.*"

"Signs, Chase."

13

Bristol had knocked repeatedly, a little louder each time. So, receiving no answer, she decided to open the door and peer inside. What she saw alarmed her. Doberman was whimpering, writhing, his body contorted and twisted into the bedsheets. Concerned, she walked into the room and edged her way to the bed. Uncertain what to do, if anything, she stood there watching. His eyes had overflowed with tears. His muddled sobs came in sporadic bursts like swells of a storm. Inarticulate growls transitioned into a desperate prolonged pleading cry.

"Doberman?" Bristol said softly. "Doberman, wake up."

With a shout, he lurched forward. Bristol stepped backward.

"Dayle? Is that you—"

"I'm Bristol."

"Bristol?" His bewilderment faded. He wiped his eyes with an embarrassed smile, then uncoiled himself from the twisted bedding, sat against the headboard, then stroked his beard. "How long have you been standing here?"

"Not long. Why were you crying?"

"It was a bad dream. We all have them."

"Not like that."

"Why? What did I say?"

"Who's Dayle?"

Doberman rubbed his beard. "Is it time for breakfast?"

"Why did you think I was someone else?"

"Our minds. They play tricks."

"There's a man waiting in our house. He asked to see you."

"Who is he?"

"I forget his name. I think he's a lawyer."

"What does he want?"

"It's about the accident."

"I don't want to see an attorney. Tell him to go away."

There was a tapping on the door. A man poked his head inside. "It's not that simple. Mr—?"

"Doberman," said Bristol. "I told you already."

"Mr. Doberman, I—"

"Just Doberman," said Doberman.

"Justin, did you say?"

"No. What is it you want?"

"I'm the agent representing the insurance company. My name's Bernard Williams."

"What insurance company? I don't know—"

"The man whose car hit you. The insured. We represent him."

"I'm not going to sue, if that's what you came to ask."

Bernard came closer to unclasp an attache case and pull out sheets of paper. "Welcome news. But the hospital that treated you, they want his money. And they intend to collect. To be reimbursed for your hospital care and 3-day visit."

"Deal directly with them."

"We are. But Medi-Cal requires a social security number. For the paper work, legally required by the government, in order to settle the claim. Now, if you'd please provide for me—"

"I don't have one."

"If you've forgotten your number we can—"

"All I want, is to be left alone."

"I'm afraid that is no longer an option, Justin."

"It's Doberman. I carry no identification."

"We have other means at our disposal to recover—"

"I lost everything! I have nothing! Go away."

"If you refuse to comply, there are statutory laws requiring that you do. Penalties can be brought against you. Which will most likely lead to a criminal charge, your arrest, and incarceration."

"For being hit by a car? That ran a red light! Illegally!"

There was a scuffling noise outside the door, which swung open. Another man was there. He, too, wore a business suit. Daleka was behind him and pushed past into the room.

"This man, he ask to see you. I tell him to leave. He does. Then sneak around back of house. I call police, yes?"

Doberman rubbed his eyes. "Who the hell are you?"

"Do not sign or do *anything*. Consult with me first."

"Again, you *are?*"

"Steven Douglas." He handed Doberman his business card and gave a curt laugh. "I know. Two first names. I answer to both. Steve or Doug. Personal injury attorney. At your service."

"I didn't ask for your assistance."

"But someone at the hospital thought you might need some."

"Who?"

"Does it matter? I'm here. You've a solid case for a civil action lawsuit. You are entitled to a substantial monetary compensation for your pain and suffering. And for your future loss of income."

"I'm homeless."

"Ah, that is not what I'm seeing," said Douglas.

Doberman countered, "Also unemployed."

Douglas rubbed his palms. "I'm talking about *future* income loss. There's a difference. And there is no reason to think—"

"Now listen here, Douglas, or Steven," said Williams. "I was in the middle of a conversation with this man before—"

"Before he had legal representation," stated Douglas.

"Good *God*," groaned Doberman.

Mozart had wandered into the room to observe the two men arguing and haggling. Doberman shut his eyes, before reopening and refocusing on all attendees in the overcrowded room. He looked at Daleka, expressing guilt.

"My fault. I get them to leave. Call Mr. Sparks?"

"No. I'll deal with this." He looked squarely at Bristol. "Please, will you promise me you'll never cross the street again without first looking both ways?"

"I promise."

"As for you two. Go. Arrest me. Take me to court. I don't care one way or the other. I have nothing more to say."

"You're making a foolish mistake," said Douglas.

"It wouldn't be my first."

"Mark my words, Mr. Doberman—"

"It's just Doberman!"

"You have not seen the last of me, I can assure you."

"Please go."

14

Norm approached Chase in the hallway one morning before the first class of the day.

"I have good news. You were voted in last night."

"Into what?"

"You *know* what. Wolverines."

"Your club."

"Seriously. You even got Derick's vote."

"What about Jake?"

"Does it matter? You're *in*."

Chase smiled, accepting this to be another Sign.

"What now?"

"You get initiated. It's no big deal."

Chase found himself herded with four other guys he knew from football who were also being inducted into this nebulous adolescent organization deemed illegal by the school's administrative board. He could barely see inside the full-headed Halloween mask resembling a wolf. The initiation required they run bare naked (except for a jock strap) a quarter mile along the street where the congestion of buses and cars existed after school. The episode was captured on cellphone videos by several students. The purpose behind the ritual of wearing the wolf masks was: 1) to symbolically recognize their club, and 2) to conceal the identity of the miscreants who were involved.

The founder's conceptual plan had proven effective until Chase, because of the uniquely identifiable fractal scar across his chest.

In the dean's office, Chase was interrogated for his involvement and misconduct. He was instructed to write down the names of all the Wolverines members. He refused and was suspended from school for three weeks and placed on probation for a year.

⸺⸺⸺

Three weeks later, Chase was riding in the backseat of Jake's restored 1969 Boss 429 Mustang. Julia Winston was sitting beside him while Kay Foster rode shotgun in the bucket seat next to Jake. They were on their way to a party hosted by Norm, whose parents were out of town for the weekend.

"I thought you'd crack, Chase," said Jake, glancing in the rear view mirror. "You proved yourself to be solid."

"He only looks cracked," Kay joked. "Love the scar, Chase."

"And your buns too," said Jules.

They all laughed.

Jake added, "I figured for sure you'd give us all up. I was wrong. Norm was right about you."

Chase shrugged. "The dean wanted me to write down what he already knows. I just refused to play his cat and mouse game."

"Thanks," said Jake. "For not being a rat."

Kay turned to look between the bucket seats. "Did you see that sign coming, Chase?"

He shook his head, questioning her skewed smile.

Jake passed Kay the flask of vodka. She lowered her head, took a sip, and handed it to Jules. "*Signs*. He receives them."

Jules drank from the flask then withheld it, directing her playful frown at Chase. "Explain yourself, *mister*. Signs?"

"It's stupid. It's nothing," said Chase.

"Uh-*uh*," urged Kay. "*Something*. Tell them, Chase. It's cool. You're among friends. Confess!"

Kay was getting drunk, Chase realized, and carelessly breaching their bond of trust and spilling his divulged secrets.

"Yeah, confess," said Jake, glancing backwards.

Chase took the flask from Jules, swallowed vodka, then placed it back into Jake's hand.

"After being struck by lightning," Kay said, "he's been getting these *signs* from God. Seriously."

"Bullshit," laughed Jake. "Tell me you're joking."

Chase glared at Kay's inebriated grin. "Yeah, it's a joke."

"Come on, Chase," said Kay, turning her eyes on him and then at Jules. "No joke. Okay, you're strange. But cool. It's why he signed up to be in The Wizard of Oz last year. And it's why he decided to play football *this* year. Tell them I'm right. Admit it."

"You're drunk," said Chase.

"*May-be.*"

Kay and Jules both laughed.

"Party time." Jake slowed to a stop behind a row of parked cars on a suburban street. He revved the engine before killing it. He gave Chase a backward glance and a laugh. "Hey, whatever. You think I really care? Norm already told me you were weird."

———

Chase was peeved at Kay as he walked into Norm's house. The party was in full bloom. No one there was of legal drinking age but there was no apparent shortage of alcohol. Chase was wearing his Wolverines jacket, an article handed down by past members who had graduated. The wool-and-leather bomber jacket was black with their club name embroidered in green letters across the back.

Norm approached Chase and handed him a can of beer.

"Free at last!" he joked. "How was house arrest?"

"My parents will get over this blotch on my stellar record."

Chase watched Jules and Kay merge into the crowd with Jake, going outside to mingle by the pool.

A few students came over to congratulate Chase. Norm toasted him. "You're a legend, my friend. Hit by lightning. Defied the dean. Suspended from school. What next?"

"God only knows." Chase grinned and took a swig of beer.

Realizing he was getting a reputation and one he wasn't sure he wanted, Chase excused himself to locate his date.

Signs were now everywhere. Or maybe the alcohol was talking and clarity coalescing into one big blur. Signs of meager significance. Familiar faces. Bright lights. Shouts of laughter. Exposed breasts. He stopped to admire Jenny Miller's tease of bare flesh. On a whim, or dare, she was known to lift her sweater and flash her assets.

"That's for you," she told Chase with a giggle.

Chase raised his eyebrows and smiled. He went outside, down steps to the patio area, where he found Jules and Kay chugging beers with their cheerleader friends. Chants escalated from the boys who cheered them on. Jake was among the rabble, along with Derick who saw Chase and greeted him with a pretend punch to the stomach. Instead, he softly shoved Chase in the shoulder.

"You're all right. About last year in the parking lot—"

"Forgotten," said Chase. "What's going on?"

"A challenge. To see who can drink the most in a minute."

"Who's winning?"

"Jake's girl. Every year, man, he knows how to pick 'em."

"And the victor in this chug-fest. What's she get?"

Derick looked down with a leer at Chase as if sharing a sly joke. "Exactly. It's like football. I do all the hard blocks and tackles. And Jake, he's the one who gets to score."

Chase faked a conspiratorial grin.

"I don't like the rules either, but hey," Derick laughed.

When Kay won the contest there were cheers. Jules saw Chase and came over to lock arms with him. "Boo-hoo, me. I lost."

"Don't be sad. Sometimes you're better off losing."

Jules kissed him on the cheek. "You *are* weird. Come on, let's go have some fun inside."

Norm's parents had a game room. An hour later, after shooting pool, playing air hockey, and throwing darts, Chase looked around but hadn't seen Kay nor Jake enter.

"I need to use the bathroom," he told Jules.

Chase walked around the party goers gathered in rooms on the main floor, stepped outside to look around, then ventured upstairs to search for Kay. The long hallway felt eerily quiet. He checked each room. He eventually came to a door where he heard activity coming from inside. There was laughter.

Chase opened the door and walked in. He recognized students who had graduated last year, and two seniors, including Jake. They were all standing around. "What's up?"

An older guy he didn't know turned and said, "Beat it."

"He's okay," said Jake.

Chase saw they were in a bedroom, and behind them was a girl lying on the bed. It was Kay.

"What happened?"

"Nothing," said someone.

"Yet," joked another.

"Kay passed out," said Jake. "She drank too much."

"Chicks," someone added.

Chase wedged between them to reach Kay. She lay supine across the bed, sprawled with arms at her side, her legs touching the floor. Her skirt was bunched over her waist and her panties exposed.

Chase sat down on the bed. He pulled her upright, supporting her back and head. "Kay. *Kay*, wake up."

Her eyelids lifted slowly. She smiled weakly. "Chasey. Why are

57

you here? What's going on?"

"You fell asleep. Too much to drink."

"*Oops.* Why is everyone staring funny at me?"

Kay's face changed from drunken levity to pallid distress.

"What's wrong?"

"I'm … I think, going to be sick."

Chase said, "Quick, help me get her to the bathroom!"

Everyone backed away except for Jake who grabbed Kay's other side as they both rapidly ushered her into the adjoining bathroom. Chase flipped up the toilet seat just in time for Kay's head to lower and vomit into the bowl.

"Gross," someone said from the doorway.

"I'm out of here," said a voice. "Let's go."

Jake stood up. Chase stayed crouched next to Kay. He held her by the shoulder. His other hand kept her long hair from falling into her face and the toilet.

He looked up at Jake. "It's okay. I've got this."

"Be my guest. I'll be outside."

Kay paused to groan, lifting her head, before lurching forward again to heave up more of her insides. Several minutes later, she was gagging, with nothing left to vomit, but had dropped from her knees to her side and was holding the sides of the toilet.

Chase found a wash cloth and soaked it with hot water from the sink. He wiped Kay's face, then dried her skin with a hand towel, before helping her stand.

Embarrassed, she refused to look at him.

"Hey," he said, lifting her chin. "You're going to live."

Kay laughed and hugged him.

15

Doberman felt a gentle tug on his right hand. It was extended beyond the sheets from the bed.

"Get up, Doberman," said Bristol.

"Let me sleep."

"It's almost noon. You sleep too much. Come outside."

"I've been outside. For more than a year."

"It's a beautiful day. Five days before Christmas."

Doberman flinched and pulled his arm beneath the covers.

"Stop being sad. Why *are* you so sad?"

He turned his back to her. "Leave me alone."

Bristol shoved his backside. "No. Teach me how you play the violin. You promised. Come on. Roll over, Doberman."

He groaned and rolled back, squinting at her.

"Good boy," she teased. "Now sit up."

His testy expression cracked into a grumpy smile.

"I'll help you get up. Give me your hand."

"I'm not going outside in these pajamas. Or in a bathrobe. It's winter. I'll be cold."

"It feels nice out." Bristol pointed behind her. "See that? A coat.

No excuses now."

A full-length parka hung over a chair. "Whose is that?"

"My dads. He's about your size. I thought Santa would be fat, but it turns out he's *not*. Surprise!"

"Funny." He pushed his body up. "That might not fit."

"Quit stalling. Give me your hand." Bristol saw the puncture marks and scars trailing up his wrist and hesitated before she asked, "What happened to your arm? Do those still hurt?"

"No. Grab my hand. Hold tight."

Doberman used Bristol to leverage his torso upright. He lifted, then slid his left leg across the bed. He scooted to the edge, stepping down with his right leg, next hoisting the thigh-to-foot cast onto the floor. Bristol let go of his hand and raised her palm.

"Wait. Let me get the parka."

Doberman placed an arm in a sleeve. He used Bristol for balance as he pulled the coat around his backside and slipped his other arm inside, then leaned back, resting against the bed.

Bristol brought the wheelchair over.

"Sit down."

"I can use the crutches."

"Sit, Doberman. I'll push you."

"You're a pushy little girl, you know that?"

Doberman sat. Bristol wheeled him out the door, down the short ramp, then over to a patio table. A violin case was on a seat.

———

"Tension," said Doberman. "That is the strange irony behind all of the amazing music this instrument can produce."

"How do you mean?" said Bristol.

"The spectrum of vibrations from coiled strings." He placed the violin to his chin. He raised the bow. "Which can be harmonious." He demonstrated. "Or discordant." He made a scraping noise.

"Lovely."

"When the bow is held lightly and the fingers shift fluidly, like so, you get good results. I'll show you spider exercises later."

"I hate spiders."

"Finger push-ups down on the palm of your other hand. It helps flex and strengthen finger muscles. Watch and listen."

Doberman played a series of notes. "See how my fingers move? The bow is meant to be kept between the bridge and the fingerboard. With practice you develop an awareness and kinetic understanding of each shift and release between notes." He demonstrated again.

"That wasn't Mozart. You told me you only knew one song. Whose music was that?"

"I used to fool around a bit. One of my creations."

"I love it. I want to know how to play that."

"It's magic."

"I'm serious, Doberman."

"So am I. Knowing the notes, scales and keys are essential. Sure, but there's a hidden element. Learning the names of the four strings – G, the lowest note, the next D, then A, finally E – they tell you next to nothing. These strings could just as easily have been named Moe, Larry, Shemp, and Curly."

Bristol scrunched her face.

"What? You've never heard of the Three Stooges?"

"No. Do they play the violin?"

"All dead. They were comedians. The point I'm trying to make is this: Technique is important but you need to have fun and become imaginative. To hear the music in your mind before it is even played. Knowing how to find the notes without forethought. And listening to the muse who will whisper in your ears."

"You're making no sense."

"Because it's magic. Creativity is ephemeral."

"What's that mean?"

"Fleeting."

"An example, please."

Doberman plucked on the strings by the bridge as he thought. "Ah, okay. In my garden each week I'd be watering. A hummingbird flew up one day, at arms length, hovering within the spray of water. The following week he arrived with a friend. I began whistling to them as they hovered and bathed. The next week there were more hummingbirds. Eventually, more than fifteen hummingbirds were hovering in front of me."

"Wow."

"Yes, wow. Their neon feathers – scarlet reds, emerald greens, cobalt blues – were dazzling. Somehow, we were communicating. They trusted me. I told my children, because I wanted them to see it too. So the next week I instructed my boy and girl to come outside and quietly approach. But the instant the birds saw them, they flew off, and never returned. I had lost their trust. I breached the delicate bond we had formed."

"An ephemeral one."

"It was."

"I still don't get what you're telling me."

Doberman laughed. "Nor do I. As a teacher, I'm not very good. I only know the moment was magical. The same way notes of music, arranged in a special sequence, can come to you, as if magically. It's the mystery of all creation. It arrives unexpectedly. Fleetingly."

"I didn't know you had kids."

Doberman's smile faded suddenly and fell. He handed back the violin and bow to Bristol. "Here."

"What's wrong?"

"Our lesson is over."

"What did I say?"

Doberman gripped his wheelchair and rotated it away.

"Where are you going?"

"Back inside."

Bristol stood and grabbed his wheelchair. "No."

"Let go."

"Daleka made us lunch."

"I'm not hungry."

"You have to eat." Bristol hugged Doberman around his neck, before letting go. "I liked your story. Thank you for teaching me. I want to learn how to play like you. Please don't go. Stay."

Bristol took backwards steps toward the house. Doberman kept his hands on the wheels, but didn't move. Bristol pointed at him with a playful smirk.

"I said, *stay*, Doberman."

She kept her eyes on him until his lips cracked into a smile.

Doberman sat waiting for Bristol to return. The sky was blue, the temperature mild, a slight breeze blowing. It was actually warm for a winter day. He heard a rattling noise and noticed the extention ladder. It was propped against the trunk of an oak tree. A man was climbing onto a branch to hang a string of lights.

Daleka emerged from the house. She came around the lawn and set down a tray which held glasses and a pitcher of lemonade.

"Good morning," said Doberman. "Or afternoon?"

"Yes. It is good you are out."

"Who is that?"

"Hector. He work for Mr. Sparks. Help with house. Handyman. Garden mostly."

"Do you plan to join me?"

"Yes, thank you." She sat down in a chair by the table.

"I can't believe it's winter," said Doberman.

"Why can you not?"

He indicated the blue sky and white cumulus clouds.

"Is beautiful."

"Yes, that's what I mean."

"I don't understand."

"It's not cold. But pleasant out."

"Ah, yes, I see now." Daleka smiled. She poured the lemonade into four glasses. "How do you feel today?"

"Better, thanks."

"Hector too have hard life."

Doberman took the offered lemonade. "How so?"

"He say it bad in Honduras. Father and mother jailed. Political. Gangs kill brother. Hector come with sister, hidden in trucks. Cross border on foot. Live with uncle in Diego."

"San Diego?"

"Yes. This long time ago. Legal now. Is citizen. Has wife, five young children. Very sweet."

"Does Mr. Sparks help a lot of families?"

"Yes, I think so. But, I worry."

"Why?"

She touched her forehead with her index finger. "I have, how do you say, a sick sense?"

"You mean, a sixth sense? An intuition?"

"Yes, like that. Something, I sense. Is not right."

Daleka brought her finger down to her lips. Sparks was walking toward them. He wore blue jeans and a windbreaker.

"Mind if I join you two?"

"Please," said Doberman. "After all, it is your house."

He shrugged. "We're only custodians. All of us."

"I'd say that's true," said Doberman.

"Yes, is true." Daleka handed Sparks a lemonade.

"Daleka, would you mind excusing us for a moment? I'd like to speak with Doberman alone."

"I will bring sandwiches and fruit. Get Bristol to help."

"Thanks." Sparks waited until she was further away. "Daleka's a treasure. She's been wonderful for Bristol since our family tragedy.

I couldn't have dealt with the last few years without her."

"I like Daleka."

Sparks nodded, sneezing into his napkin, then drank from his glass of lemonade. "Fighting a cold. Do you mind if we talk?"

"Have I overstayed my welcome?"

"God, no. Truth is, it's about Bristol. She's taken to you."

"She's quirky. And adorable. I've taken to her too."

Sparks smiled. He nodded in agreement, again wiping his nose apologetically. "I don't know what you've been through, Doberman, but I know it had to be awful. And I won't press you to tell me. It's partially because you put yourself in harm's way to save my daughter, but it goes deeper than that. You're an honorable man, I feel. You're a good person. Someone I can rely on?"

"I can be trusted."

"Good. You're a vet, aren't you?"

Doberman didn't respond.

"Shrapnel scars. I recognize those marks."

Doberman admitted nothing.

"Iraq? Afghanistan? It doesn't matter. The point I'm trying to make is, well, never mind. We'll talk later. Here comes our lunch."

Daleka and Bristol arrived carrying trays of food.

They ate in silence, watching the activity in the patio area.

Hector had helpers. A large truck was backing into the patio by the side of the house. Doberman asked, "What's going on?"

"For Christmas. Making house festive."

"Looks pretty elaborate. Hector does this every year?"

Daleka shook her head. "Most years."

Sparks coughed into his napkin again. "Excuse me. I'll be right back. I need to make a couple business calls. Carry on without me." He stood, took out his cell phone, and walked away.

Daleka looked at his plate. A single bite had been taken from his sandwich. "Your father needs to eat more."

"He'll be back." Bristol turned to Doberman, "When I was five, Hector didn't decorate the house. That's the year my mother and brother were killed."

"Your father told me," said Doberman. "I'm sorry."

"I don't remember much. Except being sad. We try not to talk about that time."

"Both are in heaven now. In God's house, yes?"

Daleka changed the subject by asking Bristol about decorations for the interior. Doberman munched on his sandwich and wondered about the concept of God, wishful thinking, mechanisms for coping. As he watched two men open the back doors to the truck, he heard Bristol saying something to him.

"What did you ask me?"

"Are you looking forward to Christmas—"

A sudden boom, sounding like a detonation, caused Doberman to twist and lurch violently. He fell off his wheelchair.

"Doberman!"

Daleka and Bristol helped lift him back into his chair. A look of disorientation and terror showed on his face.

"What the hell was that?"

"They're just delivering tables for the party," said Bristol.

Daleka shouted, "Hector, tell men to be quiet! Not throw tables onto ground!"

Still trembling, Doberman asked, "A party? Here?"

"My dad has a party for friends and neighbors. It's really fun. You'll like—

"I need to go back inside," said Doberman.

"What's wrong?"

"I can't be out here. Get me inside, please."

"Okay," said Daleka, "I will help you."

"It was only tables falling, Doberman," said Bristol.

"You don't understand. Bad things happen."

Daleka pushed his wheelchair.

Bristol followed behind them. "You're not making sense. What bad things happen?"

"I'm bad luck right before Christmas."

16

In the spring of his sophmore year, Chase was walking through the cafeteria at lunchtime. He had purchased bottled water to take outside. Chase now regularly brought a bag lunch and sat on the lawn with his friends. During his freshman year, when he hadn't brought his own lunch, his parents gave him money to buy cooked meals at the school food court.

He noticed a boy eating alone at the corner of the room. From a nearby table, a group of boys were laughing and chucking french fries at him. The boy kept his head down, doing his best to eat from his tray of food and ignore the intermittent interruptions from these tossed missiles. Chase stopped to observe, belatedly realizing this was the boy who had been bullied on the school bus his freshman year. The one he had attempted to help.

Chase interpreted this realization as a call to act. Instead of going outside, he went over to the boy and sat across from him. The laughs and taunts from the nearby table ceased. The boy looked up, startled by his presence. Behind his thick glasses, the boy's blue eyes blinked defensively then curiously at Chase.

"Hi, I'm—"

"I kn-n-now who you are. What d-do you want?"

"I came over to say hi," said Chase.

The boy glanced behind Chase at the table of kids who'd been harassing him. "Is this a p-p-prank?"

"What? No. My name's Chase. What's yours?"

"N-Nathan. You used to ride the b-bus."

Chase opened the paper bag and took out his sandwich. "I drive or get rides now. Riding the bus wasn't so bad."

"I c-can't wait. To get a c-car." Nathan removed a french fry from his plate as if it were a worm, setting it on the table.

"Do other kids hassle you a lot?"

Nathan scowled. "What do you think?"

"That sucks." Chase chewed. "I know what that's like."

"N-no you don't."

"You're right. It's not the same. Who hassels you?"

"Your f-f-friends."

"They're not my friends. Who?"

He shook his head. "I wish I c-could be invisible."

Chase took a sip of water and smiled "*Just* invisible. Seriously? Nathan, you realize people would still hear your stutter."

Nathan laughed.

Chase saw the leather case beside his books. "What's that?"

"V-violin."

"Can you play it?"

Nathan stared at Chase. "W-why else would I have it?"

"How difficult is it to play?"

"Imp-p-possible. I like the g-guitar better."

"Acoustic or electric?"

"Both. What I like most is to s-sing."

Chase laughed, then realized he wasn't joking. "Really? That's kinda weird."

"Not as w-weird as being struck by l-lightning."

Chase smiled. "Right. Now I'm curious to hear you sing."

"N-now?"

"N-n-n-*no*," Chase joked. "But sometime."

"If you want, you c-can hear me on Sunday."

"What happens Sunday?"

Chase was seated next to Julia Winston. They sat in the pews of St. Stephen's Episcopal Church and were waiting for the service to begin. He didn't know what to expect. The last time he'd been inside a church was for his grandfather's funeral. The only other time was when his parents had placed him in a daylong program the church provided for babysitting pre-school children with the eventual hope of indoctrinating them.

His father would joke, saying, "I'm a devout agnostic Christian, meaning I don't believe in the organized religious denominations." Instead, for him, God was everywhere each day when he took nature walks or worked his garden. Which was where his father was at that moment, pruning bushes and pulling weeds. His mother told him she had an appointment attending to a client's therapeutic needs.

Chase asked Jules if she wanted to come and hear Nathan sing. Curious too, she said yes to his invitation. They idly flipped through the program and felt awkward as newcomers. The pastor delivered a sermon that wove current and past transgressions into one moral lesson which enouraged repentance. Chase shared the hymn book. He spread the pages open as they sang and mouthed along to songs that appeared to inspire the congregation. However, they did little for him. The hymnals, he felt, seemed tired and lacked imagination. Yet he appreciated the effort to rouse their communal spirit.

The choir emerged from doors on opposite sides of the pulpit. Nathan was among them and took a stand somewhere near the end. As they sang, Chase was unable to distinguish Nathan's voice from the whole. The overall harmony and rendition of Ave Maria, one of

Chase's favorite Christmas songs, was quite good, yet Nathan could have been lip-syncing the words. Upon completion, the choir turned and walked away in two single files through the back doors.

The pastor then introduced Nathan by announcing he would be singing a devotional song he had written and wished to perform. Nathan had removed his red choir robe and wore blue jeans and a tropical shirt. He walked out onto the altar with an acoustic guitar around his neck. He strummed the strings softly, a flurry of chords, which led into his song. Chase was anxious for his stuttering friend whose affliction was likely to bring public embarrassment despite his courage to perform. He glanced at Jules, who echoed his concern, and they held hands. The guitar playing had a complex yet effortless quality, producing a haunting melody, blending beautifully with his passionate lyrics. It stunned Chase. His body experienced a warm tingling chill of both relief and joy. He looked at Jules who had tears in her eyes. Nathan's un-stuttered voice was mellifluous.

Following the service, Chase and Jules stood outside and were greeted as guests by the congregation. They waited for Nathan who, upon seeing Chase, seemed surprised he would still be there.

"Hi," he said. "Thanks for c-coming."

"Nathan, this is Julia. Or Jules."

They shook hands.

"Good *God*," said Chase. "How the hell did you do that?"

Nathan was taken aback. "D-do what?"

"You sing like an angel," said Jules.

"Yeah, *that*," joked Chase.

"Oh." He blinked shyly behind his glasses. "Thanks."

"You didn't stutter even once," said Chase.

"I n-never stutter when I s-sing here."

"That's weird," said Chase.

"I k-know," laughed Nathan.

"I loved your song," said Jules. "It was so beautiful."

"You wrote that?" said Chase.

"Yeah. D-do you want to hear more?"

———

Chase had recently acquired his driver's licence. At age sixteen, he wasn't permitted (legally) to drive with more than one non-family passenger unless accompanied by a parent or guardian, so Chase was breaking the law when he gave Nathan a ride home. Because of his attendance at church, Chase rationalized that God would be more forgiving, and approve of his decision, even if the state of California did not. Nathan's invitation for Chase and Jules to hear more music at his house was an offer Chase felt he shouldn't refuse.

To a degree, Chase had recognized himself (his previous self) in Nathan's shy and reclusive personality. At home, Nathan revealed himself to be more confident, an accomplished individual struggling to emerge from his multiple insecurities.

Chased asked, "These are all yours?"

The room which Nathan led them to was filled with equipment, all relating to music. A grand piano, a variety of guitars, amplifiers, soundboards, microphones, computer workstation, recording units, drum set, and a violin (out of its case) which Chase picked up, as if magnetically drawn to it.

"You play all these instruments?"

Nathan nodded sheepishly. "N-not that well."

"Bullshit," said Chase. "I'll bet you're really good."

Jules had gravitated to the piano, an instrument she was taking lessons to learn, and tinkered on the keys. After doodling around, she turned and said, "Play something for us, Nathan."

Adjusting his glasses, he looked around while brushing back his hair compulsively as if unable to decide from too many choices. He picked up the electric guitar, then set it back on its stand. Chase and Jules watched with fascination as he moved about the room, looking at one item, then another. His expression of overwhelmed indecision suddenly switched to one of excitement.

"I want you to hear this." He went and sat at the computer and tapped on the keys. "T-tell me what you think."

Nathan pushed a button. Music filled the room from two large speakers. A song composed of piano, guitars, drums, and his voice. Both Chase and Jules sat listening. Nathan's leg bounced nervously. He squinted critically, until the song finished. At least thirty seconds passed before a word was spoken.

Jules said. "That was amazing."

Chase added, "Did you play all the instruments?"

Nathan nodded. "Was it okay?"

"Are you kidding? It was great! You wrote that?"

Nathan shrugged. "I can play more songs? If you want."

Chase's smile transitioned into a wide grin.

"What?" said Nathan.

"You didn't stutter there once. I'd keep working on that."

"I'm t-trying. S-sorry."

"Sorry for what? You're amazing."

"Amazing," Jules echoed.

Chase realized it was another sign. "Nathan, you need to sign up and perform in the school talent show this Spring."

Nathan expressed alarm. "N-no. It's d-different in church. I'd emb-barraass myself. I c-can't."

"Yes, you can, Nathan," said Chase.

"We'll support you," added Jules.

"Remember, 'The only thing to fear is fear itself.' Okay?"

"That m-makes no sense," said Nathan.

17

Bristol knocked before entering the room. She had brought her violin and bow with the hope of getting another lesson. When she saw Doberman sprawled on his back upon the bed, the tray of food untouched, and the steak knife clenched in his right hand, she set the instrument down on a chair.

She moved quietly toward him. His eyes were shut. From them, tears were streaming. His head was rolling minutely back and forth upon the pillow. He was muttering to himself as his fingers loosened then tightened around the handle of the knife. The blade was facing inward, positioned in his fist as if to stab not slice. As the knife began to lift, Bristol reached over and touched his wrist, holding it still.

Doberman's eyes opened and saw her. A startled look of shame and defeat washed over his face. His fingers unclenched and Bristol removed the knife from his hand, as if nothing was amiss.

"You didn't eat anything. Aren't you hungry?"

"No." Doberman looked away, staring at the wall.

"I forgot. You're a vegan."

Doberman looked back with a slow forming smile.

"And you're an angel."

"I wish. I brought my violin. Except you don't look like you're in a teaching mood."

Doberman shifted upward in the bed. "Interesting," he mused. "Teachable moments. Lessons to learn. Why don't you have a seat. And we can talk."

Bristol pulled a chair over to the bed and sat. "About?"

"Embarrassing moments. What are yours?"

"What does this have to do with teaching me the violin?"

"Everything. It doesn't have to be a real moment. It could be a dream you've had. For instance, standing up in your classroom to give a report and you discover you're wearing only underwear, or worse, nothing at all."

"I've never had a dream like that," said Bristol.

"It was an example. I'm guessing you know what a fable is?"

"Sure. Like the Wolf in Sheep's Clothing."

"Exactly. The stories usually involve animals who have human characteristics, in a situation with a problem or dilemma, caused by a character trait of weakness. Followed by a resolution, and a moral lesson, at the end. Or, at least, implied."

"I'm not following. The violin?"

"I'm getting to that." Doberman shifted in bed and rubbed his beard. "My most embarrassing moment? One of them happened as an adult. Shortly after I'd been discharged, honorably, from active service in the military."

"You were in the Army?"

"Marines. Anyway, the point is, I was staying overnight in the city, at a club, a hotel for active duty soldiers and veterans from all branches. I was playing a game of poker with a small group during the Army versus Navy football game, watching it on TV. Somehow our conversation turned to discussing fables. The Fox and the Crow, Tortoise and the Hare, Lion and the Mouse, and what their lessons meant, if anything."

"I know the stories," said Bristol. "So?"

"So, the people I was with *knew* I played the fiddle."

"Violin."

"Same thing, to these guys. We began challenging each other, wagering bets on the outcome of the football game. Not in monetary terms, but humiliating consequences for those who lost. And since the Marine Corps doesn't have a team but is part of the Department of the Navy, and everyone else was betting on Army, I decided to bet on Navy. And, well, Army won the game."

Bristol was showing more interest. "What did you lose?"

"Do you know the fable of the Ant and the Grasshopper?"

"I think so. The grasshopper plays his fiddle all summer while the ant works and stores food for the winter."

"Yes, then winter comes and the grasshopper is ill prepared and has to beg for food from the ants. And the moral: Work hard, plan for the future. Idle play brings want, et cetera."

"But the grasshopper ends up providing entertainment for the ants during the long winter months."

"That is Disney's happy version. Back to my tale. As a result of tossing around these fables, my wager, if I lost, was to become the grasshopper, standing on a street corner. And since it was winter, appear impoverished, playing my violin, begging, as it were."

"And did you?"

"I honored my bet and played my fiddle, on a street corner."

"You said this was a teachable moment. What did you learn?"

"Not to make bets."

Bristol giggled. "No, really?"

"Fortitude of the human spirit."

Bristol sat back in her chair. "How do you mean?"

"Humility. It's an important lesson to learn. True to my word, I dressed as a beggar and played my violin. Fiddling away."

"But you're good. What happened?"

"People paid me no mind, oblivious to the music. A few paused to listen. Some tossed in dimes and quarters. One woman did stop, and seemed to truly enjoy my playing. She even gave me a hundred dollar bill."

"Wow."

"All the money went to charity. To the Tribute Wall."

"What's that?"

"It's a fund for fallen soldiers. For their families."

"Oh."

"Anyway, *that* was an embarrassing moment. But it was also a learning experience. The upside, you see: I became a better violinist. I wanted, more than ever, for people to take notice and appreciate the music. So I worked hard, motivated to play my best. Adversity, combined with dedication, can and *will* produce amazing results. The sad thing is this, I never imagined my life would end up a tragic replica of that day."

Bristol hesitated to ask, "What was it that caused you to end up living on the streets? It must have been difficult."

Doberman shut his eyes. "More than you can imagine."

"How did you survive?"

From his tray of untouched dinner, Doberman picked up a teriyaki chicken strip. "Fortitude of the human spirit."

18

To celebrate the holiday break, the high school put on a dance. It fell on a Friday night, three days before Christmas. Chase was on the dance floor with Jules. Kay was with Jake, who had graduated, attending a nearby university, and had returned as her date. Among their group were other Wolverines, including Norm and his date.

During the evening, the DJ switched from his playlist of current songs and played the Fifties tune, *Rock Around the Clock*. Between rehearsals for The Wizard of Oz freshman year, Kay and Chase had fooled around pretending to be auditioning for West Side Story by performing the Dance at the Gym. So, for this golden-oldie song, Chase and Kay demonstrated for their friends, doing an impromptu jitterbug, with lifts, swings, and twirls. While being encouraged with claps and laughter, Chase collided with another dancer.

Knocked down, the boy rose and lunged – tackling Chase to the floor. A fight broke out. Derick grabbed and lifted the other student off Chase and pushed him away.

The aggressor glared at Chase. "God-damned Werewolves! You did that on purpose!"

"Hey, man, it was an accident. Chill out," said Chase.

Derick pushed the other guy. "You want to fight? Try me."

"I know you. You're the asshole who broke our quarterback's collar bone last year."

"It's called tackle football," said Derick. "Your name's Stan or something. What the hell are you doing at our school?"

Stan's date tugged at his arm. "Let's go."

"Yeah, go," said Norm. "Go home to the Lost Raiders."

Derick taunted with a laugh. "How'd you guys come up with such a lame name for your club?"

"That's a laugh. Coming from a feral mutt." He pulled out a cell phone, poked numbers, and held it up to his ear."

Derick said, "Are you calling mommy?"

Chase tried to placate. "Let's call a truce. It's Christmas."

"Go to hell," said Stan. "The parking lot. After the dance."

"You're on," said Derick.

Chase wanted no part of violence. But once the dance was over, he had little choice but to enter the parking lot since their cars were there. He told Jules it might be a bluff. But if not, he'd try to stop a fight. She went to sit and wait in his car.

Norm, Derick, Jake and a few others, with Chase, waited for the other attendees of the dance to drive off. After several minutes, the parking area was quiet. It appeared to be a false alarm. They were about to leave when a car sped into the lot and screeched to a stop a short distance away. The passengers were all in shadow.

The driver spoke. "Hey, tough guy. I hear you want a fight. You've seen the movie, haven't you?"

Derick stepped forward. "The hell are you talking about?"

"Raiders of the Lost Ark. That's how we got our name."

Jake said, "You planning on getting out of the car?"

"Nah. Why use fists, or knives, at a gun fight?"

The driver stuck his arm out the open window and shot Derick in the stomach, then drove off.

Derick dropped to the pavement.

Chase shouted at Jules, "Call 911!" He ran over to Derick with Norm and the others.

Derick lay on his back with blood seeping through his shirt. He was moaning, "I can't move my legs."

Christmas and New Years Eve were over by the time Derick was released from the hospital. Chase had made several trips to visit him at the medical center, but he had never before entered Derick's home. He rang the bell. The door opened.

"Hi," said Chase, "I'm here to see Derick."

"Why?" The woman looked at him with accusing eyes.

"I'm a friend."

"One of his *Wolverine* friends?"

"May I come in?"

"I don't see what good it'll do. He's sulking in his room. Third door down the hall to the right."

"Thank you." Chase stepped inside and faced a large man who approached him from the living room. "Hello, Sir. I'm Chase."

His extended hand received no greeting. The father, he assumed, looked him over as he smoked his cigarette, then shook his head and walked away, saying, "Ten minutes with the gimp, then leave."

Chase followed the mother's directions. Knocking on the door, but not hearing a reply, he entered. "Derick?"

Derick sat in a wheelchair, stiff as a statue.

Chase approached, sat on the bed. An awkward silence lasted too long for comfort. "I guess it's stupid of me to ask you how you're doing. But how are you?"

Derick scowled. "How do you think?"

"What did the physical therapists say?"

"That I'll live. I'd rather die."

"Don't say that. There's still hope."

Derick fought at tears that trickled down his face.

"At the hospital, the doctor told me the bullet traumatized the spine but didn't severe the spinal cord. The paralysis might not be permanent. Sensation could return. How much do you feel?"

"What difference does it make? I'll never be the same."

"You don't know that for sure."

"Thanks for cheering me up, Chase. If you're not willing to end my misery with a bullet, why don't you just get out of here."

As Derick turned his wheelchair away, Chase saw the bruises on the side of this friend's head.

"Those marks on your face? How'd that happen?"

Derick glared back. "You really want to know? My father. He beats me. Calls me names. Cripple. Gimp. Loser. Which is what I am. Pathetic. I'm helpless, Chase. I can't even defend myself!"

Derick looked away, stifling sobs.

Chase stood, trembling with anger. "Derick, my mother, she's a therapist. My father works for the government. He knows people in social services. I think I can get him to find you help."

"Please. Get me out of this hellhole."

Chase was expelled. The dean saw to it. A Wolverines jacket was in his car. Flasks of liquor were also found. Not in Chase's car, but that didn't matter. Chase had been suspended, was on probation, and the dean wanted him gone, to be used as a scapegoat to ward off delinquent behavior among students attending his school.

At age seventeen, Chase joined the Marines. Without a diploma, he was required to pass General Education Development (GED) tests and receive a certificate proving he had high-school level academic skills. Prior to joining the military, Chase made sure his parents had set the gears in motion to help Derick escape his home environment. He kissed Jules goodbye, asking her to write him, and she promised she would. He then went off to boot camp.

Phase One of basic training was a psychological dismantling of his civilian mindset intended to instill the needed mental as well as physical qualities to function under stress. Phase Two taught Chase field skills and marksmanship. Phase Three honed his combat skills and tested him on his abilities. After the graduation ceremony, Chase was allowed a ten-day leave before he was shipped overseas to fight in Afghanistan.

During his first 18-month tour of duty, he received letters from Jules, as she promised, informing him of local news and expressing her love. Derick was living in a group housing facility and receiving an experimental therapy treatment to regenerate the nerve damage to his spinal cord. There were hopeful signs he might regain partial use of his legs. Norm had gone off to college. Kay married Jake after her graduation, then filed for divorce three months later citing physical and psychological abuse. Her whereabouts had become unknown. Ashamed and embarrassed by this failure, Kay told Jules, "I'll be moving to somewhere as far away as possible."

Chase proposed to Julia when he returned home. On his 30-day leave, they married at City Hall, honeymooned at a coastal cottage, and made love on the beach. Upon the sand, they felt inseparable, sharing their deepest feelings. Jules told Chase she had always loved the ocean, for it was where life began. It held the universal voice. Whether calm or rough, it was everpresent, and beautiful, like their love, sometimes far away but never apart.

Chase was next deployed to Iraq. He received constant letters from Jules and occasional notes from his mother. One informed him that his parents were moving to a retirement community. His father had been diagnosed with Alzheimers. When Chase returned home on leave, his father was unable to recognize his son. His mother by then had stoically accepted this cataclysmic shift and moved on with her life, she claimed. Behind a cheerful facade, she celebrated Christmas with Chase and Jules before he returned to serve overseas in Iraq.

On his last tour of active duty, Chase was the turret gunner in the third Humvee in a convoy moving down a desolate road. Desert was on both sides for miles and the buildings they were approaching were in ruins from bombings. Stationed atop the vehicle, Chase was communicating with Reynolds, their driver, and Murphy, who rode shotgun, and Rudner, seated in the back, talking into the headgear intercom system to break up the boredom.

Murphy: "I don't like the looks of this place."

Chase: "Few places around these parts are here to like us."

Reynolds: "I'm getting a really bad vibe."

Chase: "You're not psychic, Reynolds. You're a Worry Warrior. Let's try talking about something else."

Murphy: "Okay, Chase. Your name. How'd your parents decide on calling you Tober?"

Chase: "From a distant ancestor. Tobermann, which is derived from Tober, a variant of *Tauber*, and the name of a German river. Tobermann created the Doberman Pincher breed. And he named the dog after himself, but after he had changed his name to Dobermann. To answer your question."

Reynolds laughed. "You're a god-damned pedigree, Chase."

Chase replied: "Damn right, I am."

Murphy: "Doberman. That's my new name for you."

Chase: "Hey, call me a dog, I don't care, because in three days it will be Christmas. I turn twenty-one right after the new year. And then, my friends, I'll be discharged and home free."

Murphy: "You're lucky to have a wife waiting for you."

Reynolds: "Julia was your high school sweetheart?"

Chase thought of Kay, then pictured Jules. "Yeah, she was. She knows me. I love being with her. Unlike you idiots."

Reynolds laughed: "I hope to see Jesus one day too *and* be home with my wife – but not in that particular order."

Chase: "Relax. We'll be out of here soon and back at the base. And after that, I'll be home with Jules living in Paradise."

Reynolds: "Figuratively speaking?

Chase: "Literally."

Murphy: "Any place is better than this wasteland."

Chase: "The town is actually called Paradise. It's nestled in the Sierra Nevada foothills. Rustic. Away from the cities. Trees, canyons, lakes. Paradise, my friends—"

A rocket-propelled grenade hit and exploded the lead Humvee. The warhead separated the metal into flaming parts. Three seconds later Chase was airborne. The front tire took the brunt of the missile strike and flipped their Humvee, catapulting Chase. He landed in the sand and dirt. His neck and forearms felt on fire. He saw shrapnel burns and blood, but nothing life threatening. Not like the screams he heard from their Humvee. It was on its side, on fire. He staggered back to the vehicle. The driver-side door was blown off. Rudner had pushed open the back door and was climbing out. Chase hoisted onto the remains of the side panel and saw Reynolds unconscious and strapped to his seat. Murphy was screaming with his leg on fire, unable to free himself. Chase unsnapped Reynolds' seat buckle, then yanked him from the Humvee with Rudner's help. They dragged him into a ditch. Seconds later, their vehicle was engulfed in flames.

The quiet desert had become a chaotic flurry of bullets, machine gun fire, and explosions. Reynolds' left foot was half gone, and his leg bleeding out. Chase slipped off his belt. Using it as a tourniquet, he cinched Reynolds' leg below the knee. The sound of a helicopter got Chase and Rudner waving their arms to signal the pilot.

Expecting to die, Chase helped load Reynolds into the chopper, then prayed they were not all shot down from the sky. Miraculously, they were airlifted back to the base for emergency medical treatment. Days later, Chase and Reynolds were shipped back to the States. Not the way he wanted his military service to end but, nevertheless, he received an honorable discharge and early release. His wounds were not severe, only burns and shrapnel scarring to neck and forearms, whereas Reynolds had lost his foot, amputated at the ankle and calf. Both men swore to reunite in the years to come.

With his modest pension and Jule's part time employment as a dental hygienist, Chase was able to start a woodworking business. He designed and constructed custom cabinets, decks, fences, doors, even mailboxes, or whatever the request, for whomever required his services. His attention to detail and reliability built a steady clientele. A year later, his business was thriving, at least doing well enough to begin establishing roots within this rural community.

Once Chase qualified for a VA loan, they became home owners, and soon after made plans to raise a family. Jules gave birth to a boy who they named Chet. A baby girl followed two years later. They named her Dayle. When they grew older, Chase would point out the homes and businesses he had done work for, indicating signs, doors, and fences. His children loved the mailboxes he created, on display throughout Paradise. Each design was fabricated from a variety of woods, transformed into castles, dragons, racoons, dogs and cats. Chase was called foolish, by some, for donating his services to help schools and churchs instead of profiting from his labor. The people who advised him to be more pragmatic with his time were the accountants and bankers who reviewed his ledgers and applications for loans.

Each Christmas, Chase and Jules took their kids on a long drive to search for a tree to bring home and decorate. Dayle, his youngest, had nicknamed her brother Chip, after the cartoon character, since his name was Chet, and her name rhymed with Dale.

"Come on, Chipmunks," Chase would shout. "We're off to find the perfect tree!"

A week before Christmas, Chase helped Chet, age 9, and Dayle, age 7, rehearse for the church pageant. His son was dressed in a robe and crown as one of the three wise men. His daughter was an angel, with wings and halo. In the room behind the altar, both his children were fidgeting, afraid of go on stage. After a hug and a kiss, he told them both: "No fear. Only love. Now—go break a leg!"

They laughed and went on to perform. Brilliantly, he believed, proudly watching them in the audience with Jules. He captured the moment, like so many, on video. Chase and Jules had documented their children's early growth and the milestones, such as first words and first steps. They now had videos archived and displayed next to the family photos on the walls and on shelves. Their entire home had been renovated with elaborate woodwork he had custom-designed.

Each year his kids would moan, not wanting him to leave, but Chase made an annual trip to the city, for one day only, on the third day before Christmas.

"Chipmunks, I'll be back before you know I was gone."

Chase left at three in the morning for the drive to San Francisco. He stayed overnight at the Marines' Memorial Club where he met Reynolds and others. They reunited to honor the fallen soldiers who had died that fateful day before Christmas. As he was leaving town, Chase saw the sign. A sign he had seen many times before. But for some inexplicable reason the words gave him an eerie chill: *You Are Now Leaving Paradise.*

He reached his destination before dawn, checked into his room, then went to pay his respects at the Tribute Memorial Wall. He knew where to find each plaque, rubbing his hand over the black marble of each gold-engraved name. The date of their deaths the same. His cell phone buzzed. He saw Jules' name and poked Accept.

The sound of his children screaming sent him into panic mode. Something was horribly wrong.

"Jules, what's happening?"

"Fires! Chase, it's everywhere!"

"Where are you?"

"In our car. On the road. Evacuating."

"Daddy, help! I don't want to die!" His children were crying in the background. Chase turned in circles, wanting to do something, but unable to do anything to help.

"Cars are bursting into flames!"

"Jules!"

"Oh, God! We're not going to make it out. I love you—"

The call ended abruptly.

Chase ran upstairs to the Leatherneck bar. The television was on and people were gathered, watching the breaking news of wildfires in Butte County raging out of control, driven by fierce winds, blazing across miles at an alarming speed.

Chase immediately checked out of the hotel, reclaimed his car, and drove as fast as he could to reach his family.

The police and fire department were restricting entrance into Paradise which, by the time he arrived, was no more. He couldn't locate his family at any of the shelters. He didn't know what to do, couldn't sleep, waiting and hoping for a miracle. Days later, with the body count rising, Chase was allowed to drive to what was once his community. He stopped his car upon seeing the burned-out husks of vehicles lining the road. He got out and walked, inspecting each car, looking for Jules' Honda. The metal carcasses were unrecognizable. He looked for license plates, but they had all been removed.

An inner voice told Chase his wife and children were dead. All that remained were charred trees, twisted metal, and shards of glass. The whole town looked as if a bomb had annihilated the place. The homes which once were, were now rubble and ash. He finally found his street, then the remnants of his house. He shuffled through the snow-flurry of ash and gazed around, stupified. He realized he was standing where their garden used to be.

Chase fell to his knees, weakened by the total loss. The flowers, trees, and homes had all dissolved into a cadaverous stench of debris.

He remembered watering roses in the same spot that was now filth. Hummingbirds had gathered to hover like a rainbow in the spray. He had wanted to show his children the magic and beauty of it all. An extraordinary sight. All gone. Never to return.

Chase began to sob. Mumbled prayers escalated into rage.

"I believed. I *trusted* you. Why? God, please. Let them be alive. *Please*. Damn it! I hate you! Sorry, I'm *sorry*. Forgive me. I'm talking to myself. There is no god. Is there? It's all a lie. There never was. You don't exist! If you did, you'd kill me! *Kill me!*"

19

Doberman heard people talking. Faraway voices. There were sirens wailing. He was being grabbed and restrained. He wasn't sure where he was and didn't care. On his back. When he tried to move, he couldn't lift his arms. His wrists were tied to a bed.

Once released, he drifted. He drove to the beach. He unscrewed both license plates off his car. He carried them across the sand, along with his registration and wallet. Holding drivers license and credit cards, he threw them all into the sea. He shouted at the waves as they roared back, thundering, crashing up the shore to engulf him.

Drowning, he decided, was too easy. He wanted a slow death. He wanted to suffer. He wanted to prove there was no god to save him from himself.

"*Wake up.*"

Doberman's body was being shaken. He opened his eyes.

The recognition perplexed him. The doctor from the emergency room was sitting on his bed. Her bedside manners were strange. She surprised him further by touching the bridge of his nose.

"Does that still hurt?"

"The accident never injured my nose."

"Are you sure about that, Toto?"

Doberman pulled away. Peering at this woman, at the features of her face, he questioned her with a single word: "Kay?" Followed by another: "Foster?"

"It's Evans now. What happened to you, Chase?"

"You became a doctor."

"Good guess."

He was still stunned. "How did you know it was me?"

"Who else has a fractal scar across their chest?"

"You knew all this time?"

"Since the night of the accident. What threw me, for a moment, was your prematurely grey hair and white beard. We're only thirty-six years old. What the hell happened to you?"

"Stress. Shock. Awe. I don't recommend it."

"What are the odds we'd meet again, and like this?"

"A million to one?"

"Maybe less." Kay smiled.

"Who have you told?"

"No one. Except David. He needed to know you were a good person. But I kept your identity vague. Because I didn't know what had happened to you. And still don't."

"Jules told me you had disappeared."

"Maine. Which is like disappearing. I've been married twice. Divorced the same number. I have a boy. He's eleven."

"He lives with you?"

"Of course."

"What's his name?"

"Milo."

Chase smiled. "Nice name."

"I'm worried about you. Both David and his daughter have been giving me updates. Bristol called me yesterday. She was afraid you were going to hurt yourself."

Doberman clenched his teeth. "She had no right—"

"She cares about you. So do I."

A silence fell as they studied each other.

"Doberman?"

"What?"

"That name. Why?"

"It's a long story."

Kay put her hand on his chest. "I lost touch with Jules. That was my fault. I'd heard you two were living in California."

"Paradise." He grimaced. "What a *sick* joke. Life is cruel."

"Not always." Kay touched his hand. "That doesn't sound like the Chase I remember."

"He's dead. He died with Jules and my kids."

"Tell me about them."

"I can't. They were burned alive."

Kay squeezed his hand. "I know. Bristol told me you're afraid of going outside. And that it has something to do with the party they're having tomorrow night."

"I'm bad luck."

"That's not possible."

"Tell that to Derick, shot and paralyzed. Or my unit, ambushed in Iraq. Most of them died. Or my wife and kids, and all the others, who lived in Paradise. Dead. Three days before Christmas."

"That's what's worrying you?"

"Kay, trust me. Bad things happen."

"You saved Bristol's life. Good things happen too."

"That's different."

"Why?"

"I don't know. It just is."

"I'm coming to the party. I was invited. So I expect you to make an appearance too. You can't stay in bed forever. The world is not going to end if you come outside."

"How do you know?"

Kay pinched his nose.

"Ouch."

"Because I'm Dorothy and you are Toto. And when I come here to pick you up tomorrow night, you will follow me out, and we will have a good time. Okay?"

Kay got off the bed and started to leave.

"I don't even have a single photo. Nothing."

Kay looked back, questioning his words.

"All the movies Jules and I took. Burned up in the fire. It feels, at times, like they never existed. Like it wasn't real."

Kay felt his sadness. "It was real. Jules was the love of your life. You were meant to have children. A beautiful boy and girl. Nothing can take that away. You experienced their love. And they still exist. They live in your heart, Chase. Always."

He pulled at his beard. Tears were shimmering in his eyes as he placed two fingers against his lips.

Kay responded by kissing her fingertips. "You too. I will see you tomorrow night. Be ready."

Doberman heard the activity growing outside. Through the two windows he saw the colorful lights that Hector had strung along the roof of the main house and within the oak trees. Despite Bristol's insistence that he come to the party, he had remained in bed, except to use the bathroom. When the girl returned to take away his dinner tray, she had brought her father's long red parka and placed it on the chair for him to wear.

Outside his door he heard a shuffling noise and talking, before the knock came, and in walked Bristol followed by three other kids, two girls and one boy, around her age. Bristol was dressed in a green-and-white elfish outfit, similar to the one Doberman had seen her wearing the night of the accident. She held something red and white in her hand. It was a Santa Claus hat.

"I came to show you off." With a mischievous grin, she walked toward him. "These are my friends. I wanted them to meet Santa." She placed the hat on his head.

"Very funny." Doberman was seated in bed against pillows.

She said, "You don't mind, do you?"

"Would it matter?"

"Are you really Santa Claus?"

The girl who asked had a straight face before they all burst into giggles of laughter.

Doberman assessed their motives, rubbing his beard "Well, that depends. Are you being naughty or nice?"

"You have a broken leg," said the boy, pointing to the cast.

"It's my excuse not to be jolly this year."

"Does that mean you can't drive your sleigh?

Bristol giggled. "Sorry, Doberman. We're just having fun."

"I know. Me too."

"Except you sound kinda grumpy," said the boy.

"Put on the red coat," said Bristol. "Come outside. That will cheer you up."

"It's better if I stay away. Inside. Trust me."

There was another knock. Kay entered the cottage. She wore a black leather coat over a festive red dress and scarf. She gave him a disapproving pout.

"Why are you still in bed?"

"That's what I said too," said Bristol.

"There's someone here who wants to see you," said Kay.

A police officer in uniform stepped inside.

Doberman stiffened. "Great. Are you here to arrest me?"

"Kay tracked me down. Don't you remember me?"

"Is this about the accident insurance?"

"I'm a motorcycle cop, Chase. It's Derick."

The slow recognition became a shock. "Derick Crowley?"

"The same."

"You're walking. Standing."

"And *you* are not. What's up with that, Toto?"

"Toto?" asked Bristol.

"This guy, right here," said Derick, "I owe a debt of gratitude. He motivated me to never give up. And now I'm walking again."

Bristol said, "What happened?"

"I was shot. Paralyzed. I wanted to die. Chase wouldn't let me. He had his parents, may they rest in peace, help me to escape a bad situation. You joined the Marines, they said. You went to Iraq?"

"Afghanistan too."

"And you married Jules?"

Doberman returned a curt nod.

"What the hell happened to you, Chase?"

"It's a long story."

Sudden shrieks came from Bristol and her friends.

Alarmed, Doberman saw another man enter the room.

"Oh, my God!" Bristol grabbed hands with the other two girls. "I can't believe it's you! Are you really him?"

The man had a confident yet sheepish demeanor. He nodded at Bristol and her friends, then approached the bed.

"Am I supposed to know you?"

Bristol blurted out, "Are you *kidding* me, Doberman?"

"Doberman?" said the man.

"Nathan *Niles*," said Bristol. "He's like—you're like—"

"Famous," the boy interjected.

"Musician," said Bristol. "Pop star? Grammy winner!"

Doberman was still at a loss. "Sorry, I've been out of touch with all things current for the last—"

"N-N-Nathan. Does that help?"

Doberman shifted up in bed. "Nathan from high school? Wait,

but, I thought. Wasn't your name Nielson?"

"Stage name. Same guy."

"You look different. You wore glasses. And used to stutter."

"Still do, every now and then. I wouldn't have recognized you either, with that ridiculous white beard."

"How do you know Doberman?" said Bristol.

"Who's Doberman?"

"Stage name," said Chase.

Nathan told Bristol, "When I was about your age, a little older, I was extremely depressed. I was on the verge of committing suicide. And I might have. But Chase unexpectedly befriended me and, to put it bluntly, he saved my life."

"He saved my life too," said Bristol.

"That sounds like Chase. Why are you lying in bed?"

Doberman pointed at the leg cast.

"There's a party going on outside, I'm told," said Nathan.

"Are you going to sing?" said Bristol.

Nathan looked at his old friend. "I will, on one condition."

"*Jesus*," muttered Doberman.

———

Doberman emerged from the cottage on crutches wearing the red parka and Santa Claus hat.

Nathan smiled. "I guess I'll be singing." He left with Bristol and her friends, who followed him like an entourage as he went to get an acoustic guitar from his limousine. Derick embraced Kay with a hug and gave Chase an affectionate grip to the shoulder, "It's good to see you again. I can't stay for the party. I'm on duty. Let's stay in touch. Stay positive, my friend."

Doberman nodded, watched Derick go, then walked with Kay across the lawn. They stopped beside the rose garden which was a short distance from the patio area where the people were gathered, drinking and eating, so they could talk in private.

Kay removed a pack of cigarettes from her purse. She offered one to Chase, who shook his head. "I located Norm too. He lives in Colorado. He wanted to surprise you. But with the holidays and all. He's married, has a boy, another on the way. He said to tell you he's glad you're alive." She raised her eyebrows, lit a cigarette. "You see? The sign-up sheet in support of you living is growing."

Chase grimaced. "Those will kill you."

"That's what everyone keeps saying. Can they *all* be right?"

He huffed a laugh. "And you're a doctor?"

Kay took a last drag before flicking the cigarette into the dirt. "See, I knew you'd want to save me."

"By not telling Hector who tossed the cigarette butt, I will."

"Who?"

The shadowy shape of a dog wandered across the lawn. It came over and licked Chase's hand.

"Hector?"

"No. Mozart, say hello to Kay."

Kay watched as Chase's eyes wandered, scanning the outdoors, the display of evening lights, the colorful decorations, all the people. After his initial suspicious gaze, she detected the makings of a smile, at least a longing for one.

Chase glanced at Kay. "Do you hear that?"

"Hear what?"

"A soft hovering sound." He turned and searched the darkness of the garden behind them.

"Do you still look for signs?"

His expression hardened. "No. I'm surprised you'd even ask. What I said years ago was stupid. God is dead to me."

"If not some superstition, then what's frightening you? "

"Don't patronize me. It's real. I'm bad luck."

"Maybe there is no God, Chase, but if one exists, I don't think He, or *She*, has any control over the tragedies on earth. Bad things happen. I see it every day. Good things happen too."

"Don't lecture me, Kay."

"I'm not. I'm only trying to help."

"I'm beyond help."

Their tiff got interrupted by music. They looked toward the patio where Nathan was strumming a guitar. He then began to sing. There was a spattering of cheers and claps. People knew this song. Chase recognized it too. He recalled hearing an early recording of the music, a more complex version with drums, piano, and guitars, played for him and Jules many years ago.

As the song ended there was applause. Nathan started another. It was a Beatles' song. One that haunted.

Half of what I say is meaningless
But I say it just to reach you, Julia
Julia, Julia, ocean child, calls me
So I sing a song of love, Julia
Julia, seashell eyes, windy smile, calls me
So I sing a song of love, Julia ...

Kay looked at Chase who was fighting back tears.

"You know he chose that song for you."

"And Jules."

Doberman turned and searched the garden again.

20

Despite the absence of some tragic event occurring, Doberman remained on edge. The holiday party, three days before Christmas, had gone off without incident. The unexpected appearance of Derick and Nathan had surprised and pleased him, restoring a semblance of hope. At the party, he had ventured with Kay into the patio area to meet and mingle with the other party attendees.

The next day, David Sparks had visited the cottage to inform Doberman that Christmas Eve was a private time he wished to share exclusively with his daughter. But he invited Doberman to join them for Christmas Day. In addition, Sparks had Hector install a television in the cottage. As he worked, Hector was quiet, doing measurements and drilling holes into the wall. The two of them hadn't spoken more than a few words in passing to one another.

"Daleka told me you have a large family."

Hector looked back at Doberman with a wide grin. "My wife, she insist. Many children if we marry. How could I refuse her?"

Doberman smiled. "Handyman. That's a good thing to be. Are you also skilled working with wood?"

Uncertain of his question, Hector stopped and stared.

"Building cabinets? That sort of thing."

"Ah, sí." He placed a hand to his chest. "I love wood. All kinds. Oak, maple, walnut, cherry."

"Me too. I miss the smell. The touch and feel of it."

"What is it you do, Mr. Doberman?"

"There's no 'Mr.' It's just Doberman. Nothing. Anymore."

"You used to work with wood?"

"I did. I had a woodworking business. Making custom cabinets, doors, decks, tree houses, you name it."

"But no more?"

"No."

"That's sad. It gives me pleasure to work."

On Christmas Day, Doberman sat at the end of their dining room table to allow room for his extended left leg. All his woolen pajamas had been cut to accommodate the cast. He wore insulated slipper boots, supplied by Sparks, including the long red parka. "Consider both items holiday gifts," Sparks told him. "Besides, the coat looks better on you than me." Doberman didn't believe it, but expressed gratitude, and felt ill at ease.

Daleka, with no family of her own, was invited too. She helped cook the turkey. Sparks was to preside as the carver. Daleka boiled the potatoes. Bristol mashed them up. Doberman watched from the dining room, feeling useless, with all three of them bustling around the kitchen. He couldn't help but notice the photos framed and hung on walls, others on shelves, showing a family of four. He wanted to take a closer look, but felt it would be inappropriate.

Doberman softly drummed his fingers on the tabletop to calm his emotions running high. This holiday dinner preparation brought back memories once happy now painful. Throughout the house were Christmas decorations. Bows of holly, strings of lights, nutcrackers, and a miniature fiber-optic tree with rotating colors directly in front of him. It was situated on the island counter separating kitchen and dining room. There was also a floor-to-ceiling Christmas tree at one corner of the living room. The aftermath of presents unwrapped were under its branches.

A buzzer sounded and Bristol ran to answer the front door. Doberman wondered who it might be, expecting maybe Hector and his family. Instead, Kay and a young boy, approximately Bristol's age, entered the room. Along with the boy, Kay had also brought a basket of cookies and a bottle of red wine with a decorative bow tied around its neck. Doberman reached for his crutches to rise and greet them but Kay preempted with a smile and a touch to his shoulder to let him know it was alright to stay seated.

"This is my son, Milo. If he is not fed a cookie every hour, he will likely go berserk and destroy your house. So here."

"Really, Mom?"

Kay gave Daleka the basket of cookies and handed Sparks the wine. "For us. It has a calming effect, I'm told."

"Thank you," said Sparks. "Welcome."

Milo and Bristol stared at one another. Bristol lifted her hand in a brief wave.

"Hi," said Milo.

"I should introduce you properly," said Kay. "This is Bristol, Milo, and she's about your age."

"I'm ten," said Bristol.

"Off by one. Milo's eleven. And this is Mr. Sparks, her father, and our gracious host."

"David." Sparks extended his hand and shook Milo's.

"And Daleka. She runs the entire house. No offense."

"None taken," said Sparks.

"And – hum, what name are you going by today?"

"You choose," said Doberman.

"Santa Claus?" said Milo.

Everyone laughed.

"See," said Bristol, "Everyone *knows* your true identity."

"Bristol," said her father, "show Kay and Milo where they can put their coats.

Sparks stood to make a toast as they settled down to eat.

"May every day and every breath we take bring us closer to the understanding of love and our purpose while on this journey called life, however long or brief it may be. To all of us, who are able to be here, and to those we love who are not, but will always be present in our hearts, I pray for a Merry Christmas. This is a time to remind us of the love we should be giving all year long. Cheers."

Everyone proceeded to eat. The conversations shifted from talk about the party, to the weather, to gifts received, past and present. The dinner plates were cleared from the table by Daleka and Bristol, followed by slices of pecan pie and ice cream for dessert. The verbal exchanges drifted into silence and Kay spoke.

"Something of interest. When he was fourteen years old, Chase was struck by lightning on Christmas morning."

"Who's Chase?" said Milo.

"What are you doing?" Doberman put down his fork to stare across the table at Kay who blithely smiled and went on.

"Santa Claus. Doberman. Chase. A man of mystery who goes by many names. That Christmas morning, he received an iPod from his parents. He was wearing it when he saw a rainbow appear in the sky while a storm was passing. He ran outside to experience it and – Boom! – a lightning bolt zapped him. If he hadn't been wearing that iPod, which diverted the surge of electricity, he would have died."

"What's an iPod?" Bristol asked.

"It plays music," said Milo.

"That incident left him with a fractal scar, a strange leaf-like pattern across his chest." Kay took a sip of wine. "And *that* was how

I recognized the person who saved you, Bristol. An identifying mark which I fortunately saw in the emergency room. If it wasn't for that, I would have never guessed it was you, Chase. Your grey hair and white beard threw me off. For a man whose age is thirty-six."

"I thought you were older, "said Bristol.

"All this time," said Daleka, "you know him. Doberman?"

"We met on a school bus. First year of high school."

All eyes turned to look at Chase who rubbed his beard.

"I'd never met anyone so full of life, and optimistic."

"Doberman?" said Bristol.

"Can we *not* do this," said Chase.

Kay said, "It's Christmas. And the cat's out of the bag. You can't hide forever. Like David said when he made a toast, we're all on this journey together. And trying to understand why we exist."

"You're drunk." Chase shifted in his seat, as if to get up.

"Wrong." Kay addressed them all. "I once drank way too much. Never again. It was at a high school party. But Chase, he saved me. Didn't you?"

Bristol said, "Wait. If your real name is Chase, why do you call yourself Doberman?"

"His Christian name is Tober," said Kay. "He discarded it."

"I am confused," said Daleka.

Doberman rubbed his eyes. "Why does it matter? Tober is short for Tobermann. He was a German ancestor who changed his name to—guess what? He created the first Doberman breed and named the dog after himself. End of story."

Sparks said, "That still doesn't explain—"

"Ha, I was right!" Bristol giggled and stood. "You *are* related to a dog." She held out her hand. "Don't anyone move. Everyone stay where you are. I'll be right back."

She returned holding a small box. It was gift-wrapped in gold foil and tied with string and a bow. She walked over and set the box in front of Chase, then returned to her seat.

"A gift from me. Open it."

Embarrassed, Chase shook his head. "I can't accept this."

Bristol pouted. "Doberman, why not?"

"I shouldn't even be here. And I have nothing for you."

"Are you kidding? Not all gifts are wrapped in a box. Some gifts are just being present. Being there when it matters, Doberman."

He huffed a laugh. "How did you get to be so wise?"

"My father," said Bristol. "Now open it."

"All right, all right." At Kay, Chase said, "She's an extremely pushy little girl."

"Open it, already, Chase," said Kay.

"Who reminds me of someone else." Chase removed the ribbon, tearing off the paper. He opened the box. Inside was a silver bracelet. Attached to the thick chain was a plate engraved with a name:

DOBERMAN.

He held it up. "Is this a joke?"

Bristol giggled. "Don't you like it? Since I sorta adopted you, I thought, you know, it seemed fitting."

21

On the days following Christmas, Doberman decided he would get up and move around more, as Kay and others had recommended. He was invited by Sparks to have breakfast in the main house, which freed Bristol of her chore of bringing him food. Like a dog.

He used the alarm clock beside his bed to make sure he awoke no later than 7am. For more than a year he'd been disengaged from current events. He was disappointed to learn the political discourse, the incivility, and gridlock within the government had not changed. Avoiding the national news, he found other television channels, such as music stations to listen to while he did stretches before washing then dressing in his red parka to venture outside.

Kay came by to visit him two days after Christmas. She wanted to see how he was doing and also apologize for exposing their past history without asking his permission. She walked beside Chase as he moved slowly through the garden on his crutches.

"Are you mad at me?"

"I was. Briefly. I'm mad at myself, mostly. I should have been more forthcoming. These are good people. They deserve better."

"What you experienced was devastating."

He stopped to rest. "They've lost loved ones too."

Kay nodded sympathetically before looking at the dormant rose bushes. She touched the remnants of a rose blossom. "They needed to know you were a loving husband and father, Chase, and weren't hiding some sinister past. I'm glad you told them about Julia and your children. I know it's painful. These kinds of wounds take longer to heal."

"If ever."

She touched his hand held to his crutch. "You needed pushing. Several pushes. To get you to come out again. To start opening up."

"I'm not a flower, Kay."

"No. But we're as delicate. We only think we're strong until we realize we're not."

Chase pushed on, spiking the soil with his crutches.

Kay said, "You had to come out eventually. Were you planning on staying inside the cottage forever?"

"I had no plans."

"Will you go back to living on the streets?"

Chase stopped. "No."

"That's a plan. The makings of one. Let me help you."

"I'll figure my life out on my own."

Kay noticed a soft jangling noise as he moved. She stopped him to lift up his parka sleeve.

"You're wearing the bracelet. That's sweet."

"No. Bristol is sweet."

"And you're sour. It's a perfect match."

Chase smiled despite his moodiness. "She really is sweet. Have you ever met anyone quite like her?"

"Yes. Chase, did you ever stop to consider this."

He stopped again to look at her. "What?"

"You saved her life. It's true. But she, in turn, saved yours."

Chase asked if she had plans for New Years Eve.

"Are you asking me out?"

"Not exactly. I have no money, first of all."

"That doesn't matter, I—"

"It does to me. And I'm not ready to venture that far."

"Off your leash? Sorry."

Chase indicated his leg cast, then touched his parka. "We could celebrate here, in the patio area, if it's not raining."

"How romantic."

"Forget it. You should spend it with your son, Milo."

"I would, but he's rejected me. He was invited to a friend's party with parents who will be present, and hopefully sober, to chaperone and tamp down their inevitable coming-of-adolescent-age wildness, followed by a sleep-over. So, I'm available. And I'm not about to let you wiggle out of your invitation, Chase. I'll be here."

"Don't expect much."

"Okay, my expectations are set low. What time?"

"Eight, or nine?"

"Eight. I'll bring wine."

"I can borrow glassware from Sparks."

"Sounds like a party." She kissed him on the cheek. "I've got to run. Others are waiting to be saved in the Emergency Room. And don't be jealous, Chase. You're not my first rescue animal."

"Funny."

22

Doberman looked into the bathroom mirror and scowled, not liking what he saw. He bared his teeth. All there, fortunately, though slightly yellow, even after brushing them vigorously. He then combed back his shoulder-length grey hair. He stroked and brushed his long beard, but it remained scraggly. Searching through the tiny medicine cabinet, he found scissors. After snipping for several minutes to trim loose ends and shaping the hairs, he styled his appearance from an unkempt vagrant look to the semblance of distinguished fashion.

Who was he kidding? He looked like hell, he told himself and pushed away from the sink, hopping on one foot. He retrieved his crutches and poled his way into the bedroom. Sparks had been overly generous with the pajamas he'd purchased (with his daughter's help), all colorful with various patterns and prints. One had candy canes, the second was a mix of dogs and bones, and the third a traditional black-and-white plaid. The latter was Spark's selection, he surmised. Chase decided to wear the more formal plaid pajamas beneath the below-the-knee red parka. He then slipped on the furry boots. All gifts from Sparks.

Kay arrived, as promised, holding a bottle of red wine. She was

111

wearing the same black leather coat, red dress and scarf he had seen on her before. She looked beautiful. Chase, by contrast, looked and felt foolish. He greeted her with a smile and a hug. He ushered her on crutches to a round patio table where (with Daleka's help) he had arranged a white tablecloth with wine glasses, silverware, plates, and napkins. A candle was in a glass holder at the center of the table and already aglow.

"My expectations have risen a notch. Ah, and you've trimmed your beard."

"It didn't help. I look like a leftover Santa."

"Let me be the judge. Hum, you're right. I'm joking. Oh."

Chase pulled out a chair. Kay sat down.

"Thank you."

"It's been awhile. I'm rusty."

"You're doing fine. I think I'll keep my coat on."

The air was chilly, although not especially cold for winter. But to make sure they stayed warm, a propane heat lamp was lit nearby. Chase continued to stand as he took hold of the corkscrew.

"May I?"

"By all means." Kay smiled as he struggled to work the gadget.

"Meaning, I may have forgotten how this is done."

"You'll conquer it, I'm sure."

He did, pulling out the cork, then pouring wine into each glass. He sat and raised his glass. "What should we toast to?"

"A new year?"

"Clever. Let's start there."

They touched glasses and drank wine. Bristol and Daleka came from the house, walking toward them carrying trays. Each wore a colorful apron over festive dresses.

Kay said, "Ah, and what's this?"

"Bristol's idea," said Chase.

Using serving tongs, Bristol plucked hors d'oeuvres off the plates, serving them crackers with cream cheese topped with olives, toasted slices of bread with melted tunafish, and deviled eggs sprinkled with paprika and herbs.

Bristol bent down to fake whisper, "How's your date going?"

"Splendid," Kay laughed. "Won't you join us?"

"This dinner is for you two. We are here to serve. Maybe later. Daleka and I are playing cards until midnight comes."

"I like card games," said Kay.

"Where's your dad?" said Chase.

"Under the weather. How can you be under the weather?"

"We suspect maybe flu," said Daleka.

"Make sure he drinks lots of fluids," said Kay.

"Always the doctor," said Chase.

"Have good time, he say. Not to worry. Enjoy new year."

Bristol set down a miniature hand bell on the table. "Ring if you need us." She added, "And no funny stuff on the first date."

Doberman lifted his wrist and rattled his bracelet.

Bristol tucked her lips in to hold back a smile, then giggled and walked away with Daleka.

A couple minutes later there was soft music coming through the outside speakers. Frank Sinatra was singing:

Call me irresponsible,
Call me unreliable, throw in undependable too.
Do my foolish alibis bore you,
Well I'm not too clever - I just adore you.
Call me unpredictable - tell me I'm impractical,
Rainbows I'm inclined to pursue.
Call me irresponsible - yes I'm unreliable,
But it's undeniably true - I'm irresponsibly mad for you.

As the midnight hour approached, Chase, Kay, Bristol, and

Daleka were outside seated at the same table, now cleared of dishes, with cards in their hands playing a game of Crazy Eights. At Bristol's insistence, they each wore cone-shaped party hats in celebration of the new year. Champagne bottle confetti poppers were on the table too, ready for the moment to be pulled and popped.

"Fifteen minutes," Bristol announced and rose from her seat. "I'm going inside to wish Daddy a happy new year, then I'll be right back before it strikes midnight."

Chase, Kay, and Daleka set down their cards and watched as Bristol left. Their champagne glasses were filled with apple cider, not sparkling wine. Chase raised his glass for a sip.

It was a quiet night, except for the sounds of a few premature explosive pops from fireworks off in the distance. Then a horrifying scream. Chase dropped his glass. It crashed against the cement as he lurched in his seat, startled by the memory of his children shrieking on the phone before they died.

Bristol's screams continued, crying out for help. Daleka and Kay were quick to rise and run inside. Chase struggled with his leg cast to get upright, retrieve his crutches and get mobile.

Chase hobbled as fast as he could and followed the cries and screams coming from Bristol. Entering the bedroom, he saw Sparks lying unconscious in his bed with blood on his pillow and sheets. Kay was compressing his chest, trying to resuscitate him. Daleka was talking on a phone, giving out their address to the 911 emergency-line dispatcher. Bristol was hysterical. When she saw Doberman, she ran over and grabbed hold of his body.

As Bristol clung to Doberman, he felt her fragility. He held her tightly. He wanted to hold her heart together by telling her lies – that everything would be all right – except he couldn't. Powerless to do more than console her with an embrace, Doberman did the one thing he had refused to do for more than a year. He prayed.

23

In the hospital recovery room, David Sparks was attached to an IV as he lay in bed. He looked ashen, but alive. He smiled wanly at his daughter as he held onto her hand. Daleka was also in the room, behind Bristol. Doberman was there, too, standing at the foot of the bed. The door opened, and Kay entered.

"I've wanted to tell you," said Sparks, addressing his daughter, "but I didn't want to spoil Christmas for you. I had hoped—"

"Tell me what, Daddy?"

"After the new year, I was going—"

"To tell me *what*."

"I'm dying."

She let go of his hand. "What? You can't." She looked back at Daleka. Her eyes searched the room in the hope this was some joke, a prank, but saw only dire faces. She looked back at her father. "Tell me it's not true."

"It is, Sweetie. I'm—"

"No!" Bristol burst into tears, turned, and sunk her head into Daleka who tried to console her. "You can't die. You can't!"

Sparks spoke. "I've known for awhile I was sick."

Kay said, "It's pancreatic cancer."

Chase looked at her, "You knew about this?"

"No," said Kay. "Not until a moment ago."

"I knew," said Daleka. "But not sure. Something not right."

Sparks said, "I've been doing my best to fight it."

"What's the prognosis?" said Doberman. "That is, if you don't mind me asking?"

"Not good," said Sparks.

Kay added, "It's an aggressive cancer. I just spoke with David's oncology physician. It's metastasized to his liver and lungs."

Wiping her eyes and nose, Bristol let go of Daleka. "What does this mean, Daddy? How long? Tell me!"

"A few more weeks. It could be longer if—"

"No!" Bristol flung away from the bed. She grabbed a lamp on a table and hurled it to the floor, before throwing herself onto a chair and sobbing into its cushions. "You can't die. I'll be all alone. What's going to happen to me?"

"I've set up a trust fund."

"I don't know what that means."

"It's so you'll be provided for financially. My savings, with the money from the sale of the house, will all go to you."

Bristol raised her head. "Sell the house. Where will I live?"

"I've spoken with Mr. and Mrs. Owens, and they've agreed to take you into their family, to live with them."

"The Owens? I hate Billy Owens! No, you can't make me!" she cried and buried her face into the cushions of the chair. Suddenly, she thrust her body up and turned her head. Her eyes were full of tears, fear, and anger. She extended her arm, pointing at Doberman.

"You! You did this! You brought bad luck. You said so yourself. Bad things happen when you're around!" Bristol rose from the chair and flung herself at Doberman, flailing her arms against his body. "Get out of here! I hate you! I *hate* you!"

From the bed, Sparks raised his voice, "Bristol, stop it! This is not his fault. I knew about this before—"

"It is! Why are you even here, Doberman? Leave!"

She pushed Doberman who stumbled backwards, nearly falling. He secured his crutches and moved toward the door. "Bristol—"

"I said, get out!"

"Bristol," said Kay. "Please, calm down."

"You too! Leave!" Bristol ran and grabbed the back of the red parka as Doberman opened the door. "And leave my Daddy's coat. You can't have it! Give it back!" She pulled and tugged at the coat until he was able to let go of the handles of both crutches and extend his arms. She yanked the parka off him.

He was at a loss for words, stung by her emotional assault, not knowing what to do or say. "Bristol, I'm really sorry—"

"Go away!"

Wearing only the plaid pajamas and slippers, Doberman exited the room with the aid of his crutches. Kay followed, also shaken by the outburst. Bristol's final words were the ones that penetrated and wounded him the deepest.

"I wish I had never given you that stupid blanket!"

⸻

Doberman didn't respond, but kept moving on his crutches.

Kay said, "I'm taking you to my apartment."

She grabbed his arm to get him to stop. She could feel he was trembling and saw tears in his eyes.

"Chase, she didn't really mean what she said."

"It doesn't matter."

"Of course it does. You're coming home with me. And you can't say no. It's early morning. Still dark out. You have no where else to go. Besides, look what you're wearing."

Doberman looked down at himself, as if having forgotten he was in pajamas. He simply nodded.

Since it was New Years Day, there was no commute traffic, the freeways relatively vacant, and they reached the city and arrived at her apartment in the Marina District around six in the morning. An elevator ride took them to the third floor. Doberman remained silent the entire journey. Kay didn't ask Chase what was on his mind, because she knew he was in emotional and mental turmoil.

It was a small, two-bedroom apartment, a few blocks from the bay. Standing at the living room window, Chase could see, between the other buildings, a foggy blue-grey sky and a sliver of blood red from a tower of the Golden Gate Bridge.

"You can sleep here on the couch." Kay held a blanket and set it down.

"I'll be in your way," said Chase.

"We can manage. It's not like you'll be here forever."

"What about your son?"

"What about him?"

"Won't he mind me being here?"

"He's resilient. He might benefit from having a man around. Anyway, let me make us some coffee. Or tea?"

"Coffee, please. Thanks. For everything."

"Make yourself at home."

Kay disappeared into the kitchen. Chase stayed on his crutches, moving around to inspect the walls that had artwork. A couple small oil paintings, beachscapes, and many black-and-white photographs. A lone seagull in the sky. One of a sea lion basking on a pier. A beach empty of people on a stormy day. Fog descending the headlands like an ocean wave. A boy building a sand castle. He recognized the child as her son, a few years younger than present day.

"Are these all yours?"

She shouted from the kitchen. "Are what all mine?"

"Sorry. The photographs. They're wonderful."

She appeared with cups of coffee. "Thanks. One class in college turned me into a shutter-bug. Once infected, as they say. It's a hobby. It helps take my mind off suturing wounds." She set down the cups on a table and pivoted. "I have banana bran muffins toasting too. I'll be right back. Muffins are okay with you?"

"Kay, seriously? Whatever is fine. Thank you. Again."

To avoid the present, they were talking about the past, how they met on a bus, performed on stage, interacted during various episodes in high school, caused a fight to break out during a dance which led to the incident in the parking lot, and resulted in his expulsion.

"That was unfair. You didn't start that fight."

"The dean didn't see it that way. I don't think he liked me."

Both Kay and Chase were surprised by a voice:

"Who didn't like you?"

"Milo," said Kay, startled into a laugh. "So uncharacteristically quiet for you. I didn't hear you come in."

"Obviously. Hi."

Milo was carrying a sleeping bag and dropped it in the hallway. He greeted Chase with a curious frown when he noticed the black-and-white plaid pajamas.

Kay said, "How was the New Years Eve party?"

"Okay, I guess. I'm hungry."

"We're having muffins. I'll warm up another."

As his mother left for the kitchen, Milo wandered into the living room and sat on the sofa. He saw the blanket, and looked over at Chase.

Chase sipped his coffee. "Your mother invited me to stay for a few days."

"Okay. Why?"

"Because of what happened last night."

"What happened?"

119

"Bristol's father was rushed to the emergency room."

"Wow, that sounds bad. Is he all right?"

"No, not exactly. He's dying."

"From what? Was there some kind of accident?"

"He has cancer. It's terminal."

"Oh. That's really sad. I liked him."

Kay returned with the muffin, on a plate, along with a napkin, and gave it to her son. "Which is why Chase is staying with us."

"I'll try to stay out of everybody's way," said Chase.

"Okay," said Milo.

Kay said, "You're probably wondering about the pajamas."

"Not really." Milo bit into the muffin. He pointed. "I like these a lot better than the candy cane ones you wore on Christmas."

Chase smiled. "It was for the holidays."

"Is that something you wear mostly, pajamas?"

"Milo," said Kay.

"No," said Chase. "Fact is, I was—"

"Unable to wear much else," said Kay. "Because of his cast. But it comes off in another couple of weeks."

"Oh, yeah. Mom told me about the accident. How you saved Bristol's life."

"She may be exaggerating."

"Chase threw himself in front of a speeding car to push her out of the way. Saving her from being hit. It's not an exaggeration."

"Wow. That's awesome." Milo stuffed the last of the muffin in his mouth, stood and said, with his mouth half full. "I'm gonna take a shower. Are we doing anything today? For the New Year?"

"Maybe," said Kay. "Take your shower and we'll see."

While Milo showered, Chase and Kay resumed their talk, and shifted the conversation into present time.

Chase confessed, "I want to help her, but I'm helpless. I have no money. You need money. I'm a fool. A grasshopper."

"A what? Chase, let me help."

"I'm not about to take your money."

"You may not have to, if you let me get involved."

"Involved, how?"

"Chase, you could, and should, receive a substantial settlement payment. In the police report, the accident clearly states negligence. And it was uncontested."

"How do you know that?"

"The driver was inebriated, beyond the legal limit. There were witnesses. He nearly killed Bristol and seriously injured you."

"It feels wrong, somehow."

"His insurance company pays. It's what they're supposed to do. They compensate for damages and loss."

Chase looked away, as if pained by her words.

"What's wrong?"

"Nothing." Chase lifted his mug, finishing his coffee.

"Did you want another cup?"

"One's enough." He reached across the table to place his hand over hers. "Thank you. You're absolutely right. I needed pushing. Bristol needs my help. I need to call that attorney with the two first names. But his card is back at the cottage. Steve something?"

"Steven Douglas."

"You know him?"

"I sent him. He's awkward, but smart, and a good man."

Chase smiled and shook his head. "Knowing what I know about insurance companies, if pushed, using the right incentive, they'll be willing to settle and pay quickly, in order to avoid litigation that will likely end up costing them more. So I need to act."

"That's the Chase I remember." Kay sipped her coffee. "Don't be mad at me, but I've been meddling and discovered things you've overlooked. And it's good news."

"Tell me."

She cut into her muffin with her fork, and raised her eyebrows. "Derick helped me pull a few needed strings, so to speak."

"Derick? What does he have to do with this?"

Kay ate the slice of muffin. "You'll let me help you then? I too care about David and Bristol."

"Except that she hates me now."

"She loves you. She's in pain. You of all people should recognize the signs, Chase."

24

Three days into the new year, Chase awoke early one morning. Lying on the living room couch, he sensed he was being watched and turned his head. He found Milo sitting nearby at the dinner table. He was barefoot but wore jeans and a sweatshirt. There was a table in the kitchen used for breakfast but the boy wasn't eating anything, only sitting and staring directly at the house guest.

"Good morning," said Chase.

"Don't you have a bag?"

"Excuse me?"

"Luggage."

"Oh. Right. No."

"Nothing?"

Chase shifted up. "Not a thing. I have nothing."

Milo pointed at his pajamas.

"Not really mine. A gift from David Sparks. Bristol's father."

"A gift?"

"He graciously invited me to stay at their home. Actually, to live for awhile in their cottage."

"Why?"

"Because he was homeless." Kay stood in the hallway. She was wearing a robe over her nightgown.

Milo looked at his mother. "Homeless?"

"That's right," said Chase. "I was living on the streets."

"Why?"

"Like your mother said, I was without a home."

Milo stood and scowled at his mother. "You took in a homeless man to live with us!"

"Milo, Chase had a home. It was destroyed in a fire. He lost everything."

"How can you lose everything?"

"It's a long story." Chase shifted his body to sit upright on the couch. Sit down, Milo, and I'll tell you."

Kay walked over and sat, too. "Chase, are you sure?"

"It's time I told someone."

———

Chase began his story at the time when he was a young adult, three weeks before he turned twenty-one, stationed overseas in Iraq. When their military convoy was ambushed by anti-tank missiles. He was one of the lucky survivors. The incident had occurred three days before Christmas. And ever since, after leaving active duty, he would spend the third day before Christmas at the Marines' Memorial Club to honor his comrades who had fallen. Which happened to coincide on the same day his wife and two children were burned alive in their car while trying to escape a fast-moving wildfire that destroyed the entire town where he had lived, and had *had* a home.

"The town was called Paradise, ironically," said Chase without an ounce of humor. "I lost everything that mattered to me."

"We watched it on the news," said Kay.

"I remember," said Milo.

"Shortly afterwards, I had a psychotic breakdown."

"What's that?"

"I lost my mind. Like I said, I lost everything. I can only recall bits and pieces of that time. I was eventually incarcerated in a mental hospital. A danger to myself, they said. Once I regained a semblance of sanity and reality, I was let go."

"You went insane?"

"You could say that. Sure. Released, on my own. To wander, which is what I did. For more than a year. I had lost faith in a God, and a belief in anything. I wanted to suffer. Call it survivor's guilt. I don't know. I had no plan, really. Only that I was curious to see how long I would last before something killed me off. Maybe a mountain lion or bear. I lived in the forests. I took shelter in caves. I ate berries and drank from streams. I lost track of time but eventually ventured back into the world of urban landscapes. I begged and scrounged for food. I felt each scorn and smile of generosity I endured and received. Somehow I managed to survive. Experiencing nature's elements first-hand was a real shock to the system. Numbing yet revitalizing when the seasons changed. The bitter cold. The thaw. The warm embrace of the sun. I watched last leaves falling off spindly stems to later split open from buds showing hints of green. It was something."

"Chase?"

He looked at Kay. He nodded. "Right. Like now, my thoughts became scrambled. Vivid images too. Extremes. Sunrises as glorious as the dawn of life itself. Flickering neon lights signaling the end of time. I even imagined myself as historical, and even literary, figures. A Babylonian war refugee, Ulysses driven mad by the Sirens singing, Vincent Van Gogh as he saw the vibrant colors of the world swirling. And once a Minotaur, half bull, half man. A freak of nature."

"*Jesus*," said Milo.

Chase responded with a laugh. "Him too. I had lost all sense of self and wellbeing. Around that time a little girl startled me awake from a cold slumber that was pulling me into its abyss."

"Bristol?"

"She represented everything I had lost. Her innocence and joy caused me pain. I reacted badly – pushing her away. I doubt I'd have lasted through one more freezing night. Then I happened to look and there she was, standing on the sidewalk, happily waving, about to be run over by a car."

"Wow," said Milo. "And you saved her."

"Meaning, I shouldn't even be here. But here I am."

"That's like a miracle," Milo added.

"I have a question," said Kay.

Transitioning from past to present, Chase looked at her.

"Back at the cottage, you told me you went crazy and destroyed everything that could identify you. Car registration, license plates, wallet, and credit cards."

"So?"

"I believe you. But you also said you took all the money from your bank account, all the money you had, even tore up the check issued from the insurance company, and threw it in the ocean."

"It was stupid, I know."

"Except you didn't," said Kay.

"I did. I remember it all very vividly."

"You said yourself, you had a mental breakdown."

"What's your point?"

"Chase, you imagined half of it."

"How would you know? You weren't there."

"Why did you tear up the check from the insurance company?"

"You know why."

"Tell me."

Chase looked at Milo, still seated there too, riveted on his story. The son turned to his mother, then refocused his attention on Chase, whose teeth clenched, eyes becoming watery.

"Because it was blood money. There is no price, no amount of money that could replace what I lost. Human lives! If I'd taken the

126

money it would've been quantifying their worth."

"Chase, it was compensation to rebuild your house. The money had nothing to do with the loss of your family."

Wiping at tears, he said, "I realize that, now. I was stupid. I lost my mind. What else can I say?"

"Would you hate me if I told you the money was not gone?"

"What do you mean?"

"You deposited the check. You never tore it up."

"I did. I remember it clearly."

"The mind is strange. It plays tricks on us. Chase, I think you went crazy with guilt *because* you accepted the settlement and *after* you deposited the check into your bank account."

"That's impossible. I closed the account."

"You only imagined you did. To help free your mind of guilt. To alleviate the pain."

Chase stood, feeling a need to pace, but was hampered by his leg cast and sat back down on the couch. "That's crazy."

"You're telling me," said Kay with a restrained smile. "Do you want to know how I know this?"

"I think you're going to tell me. How?"

"First, I was shocked to realize you were the accident victim."

"The scar," said Milo.

"Uniquely identifiable. Then came the issue with the insurance companies, each wanting to know who you were. Information which you refused to give. I wanted to avoid a legal summons or threat of your arrest. And by happenstance, in my effort to wedge you out of bed and come outside, I looked up old friends. I knew about Nathan Niles, his whereabouts, and that he'd once been your friend."

"I can't believe you know him," said Milo.

"If you'd have come to the party as I'd asked, Milo, you would have seen and met him too."

"Mom, you should have insisted—"

"Milo, I *did*. It was to be kept a surprise. And it's over. Now get over it." She looked at Chase. "Back to you. I was surprised to find out Derick was around, had fully recovered, and had become a cop. So, we met, then I needled him until he agreed to bend a few rules. Once we learned your social security number, it was a matter of time before we could search and finagle the powers that be. The insurance companies have more power than I had credited them with having. We found your bank account. And verified there's money accruing. A tidy sum, waiting to be claimed. Tell me you're impressed."

"I'm impressed."

"Now," said Kay, rising from her seat. "Today we are going to go shopping for new clothes. For you. And tomorrow we enter the bank to reclaim your money. Oh, and I splurged and bought you a fashionable long parka coat similar to the one David gave you."

"In red?"

"Seasons change. Black. And you're to pay me back for all these purchases. Every penny. With the accident insurance settlement now in the works, and now this. It turns out you have way more money than I do. So there."

25

Kay remained in contact with Daleka. She had stayed in the Sparks' home to care for David, and watch over Bristol, during the remaining weeks in January. She was at his bedside when he died. A funeral had been arranged in advance, coordinated between Sparks and his attorney. Having no surviving relatives except his daughter, Sparks acquiesced, at the insistence of his close friends, and allowed there to be a memorial service for those who knew him and wished to pay their last respects.

Daleka let Chase and Kay know that David had expressed his sincere regrets with regard to his daughter's emotional outburst and expulsion of them at the hospital, and had wished to make amends before his passing. They were welcome to attend. The informal invitation left Chase and Kay somewhat apprehensive, so they remained seated in Kay's car at the church, waiting for the crowd of mourners to enter before them. Once the procession had thinned, they left the vehicle and made their way up the long steps. Kay assisted Chase, still on crutches, and they took seats in the pews toward the back.

It did not surprise Chase to see the large attendance. He felt the enormous outpouring of affection expressed for this man. The many eulogies were passionate and attested to the merits of someone who was much loved. Over the sea of heads, he caught glimpses of Bristol in front seated next to Daleka. When the service ended, he stood with Kay and watched people rise and exit down the aisle. Bristol held Daleka's hand as they led the procession.

Directly behind Bristol was a man and woman, followed by a boy and girl. Chase guessed they were the Owens family who had taken Bristol into their home to live with them. To be inconspicuous, Chase remained still, standing in the back row. He was startled when Bristol turned her head toward him. She must have noticed his beard in her peripheral vision. Chase tilted his head to express sorrow for her loss. But her face seemed void of emotion. The vibrant spark in her eyes was gone, as if the essence of life was being drained from her body. Her helpless stare caused Chase to grip the back of the pew for support.

Kay whispered, "Are you okay?"

Chase shook his head as he watched Bristol depart the church. Kay had to nudge him to move once the forward pews had cleared and it was their turn to leave. As they exited the double doors, he looked around but saw no sign of Bristol or Daleka.

At the foot of the steps he paused to readjust his crutches and said to Kay, "I swear, it was like she was drowning inside."

"Who?"

"Bristol."

"You're imagining things. It was a beautiful service."

"It was. Until I saw the look in her eyes."

"She's grieving, Chase. Give her time to heal."

They moved toward Kay's car. "It's different this time."

"Explain."

"For her. Before it's too late. We need to act soon."

Kay opened the passenger side door for Chase to get in, holding his crutches as he maneuvered into the small space of her compact sedan. Concerned by his words, she edited out her desire to ask him if this was another one of his perceived signs.

—⟨⟨⟩⟩—

Time passed. January ended, February began, and was about to transition into March. Chase was still living with Kay and her son. It was a Friday night. Milo was staying overnight at a friend's house. As the sun was setting, Chase was walking around the living room, because he could, enjoying the use of his left leg without a cast.

Kay emerged from the kitchen. "How does it feel?"

"Strangely abnormal. I feel lighter. As if I could fly."

"Keep away from the window, Superman. Here." She handed him a glass of wine. "You'll end up in a body cast. Let's sit."

Chase moved over to the couch and sat. Kay took a sip of wine and sat beside him. She set her glass on the end table and rubbed her hand over Chase's leg covered in denim jeans.

"I like you in blue. First time I've seen you in pants."

"Not the first time. High school?"

"Since your accident. We should talk about next steps."

"We should marry." Chase set down his wine glass.

"Marry?" Surprised, Kay reached for her wine. "Chase, do you realize we've never ever *once* really kissed."

He tapped her shoulder. She turned back. He leaned over, took the wine from her hand, set it on the table, and kissed her on the lips. The brief kiss was followed by a long passionate one.

"Okay. That was a kiss. And, I liked it."

"Can we marry now?"

Kay retrieved her wine. "Why can't we love each other without the formality of marriage?"

"When children are involved, we should make it legal."

Kay twisted her lips, then took a sip of wine. "Milo likes you. He'll be happy. I'm not worried about that. It's just." She pointed at his beard. "That thing has to go. Then, maybe, yes."

Daleka knocked on the front door. A woman opened it.

"Ah, you're here. Come in. Bristol is expecting you. What movie were you taking her to see?"

"Not sure, Ms. Owens. Nothing violent."

"Please, call me Darlene. Can I get you something, Delilah?"

"Daleka. Thank you, no. Only Bristol."

Standing in the foyer, Daleka heard a scream, followed by a girl, younger than Bristol, chased down the stairs by a boy. They stormed into the living room and disappeared.

"Billy! For God's sake, leave Debbie alone! Sorry." She turned back to Daleka. "Boys—*Augh*," she laughed. "Here she is."

Bristol came down the stairs. She looked sullen but smiled when she saw Daleka.

"I want her back by ten o'clock, no later. We're very strict about curfew around here."

"Yes, Ms—Darlene. Come, Bristol."

Bristol gave Daleka a hug. "Where are we going?"

"Movie, yes?"

It was now past dusk, getting dark. Once inside her car, Daleka looked over at Bristol to say, "I have missed you."

"Me too. Which movie?"

"You chose. Is good, living with Owens family?"

"It's not that horrible, I guess."

"I know. I miss my father. Mother too."

"Why are we going this way?"

"Ah, I forget. Make wrong turn. If you like, we drive by, take a look at your house."

"It's for sale," said Bristol. "And it's not mine."

As they turned the corner, Bristol rose from her slouch to get a better look. The house in which she had grown up in was decorated with Christmas lights.

"Strange, yes?"

"Why are we stopping?"

The real estate For Sale sign had the word SOLD on its top.

"Looks like new owner is fan of Christmas."

"Or crazy," said Bristol, "It's April."

"Oh, wait. Almost forgot. Realtor called to tell me owner had found something you left behind."

"I don't want it."

"Maybe important. You never know."

"You get it."

"No, you must come too. Hurry, or we miss movie."

"Whatever."

Bristol got out of the car. They both walked to the front door. A note was posted: COME INSIDE. ITEM FOR GIRL UNDER TREE.

Daleka knocked first, then opened the unlocked door."

"Hello?"

"We should come back later," said Bristol.

"See note? It's okay."

"Is anyone home?"

"Can't say. We get package, then leave."

One small box was under a lighted Christmas tree.

"That's weird. Why is it gift wrapped?"

"Don't know. Read tag."

Bristol picked up the box. "It says: 'Open Now.'"

"Do as instructed. Then we go."

Bristol tore off the paper and opened the box. Inside was a gold charm bracelet. Attached to the chain was a tiny Christmas tree, a dog, violin, painter's easel, key, and an oval plate with an engraved name, which said, BRISTOL.

"This isn't mine."

"Has your name," said Daleka. "Must be yours."

"Hello."

A man came into the room. He wore a satin vest, white dress shirt, a red tie, and black corduroy pants. His grey hair was combed back straight. His face was clean shaven.

"I didn't leave this," said Bristol. "Are you the new owner?"

"It's a belated Christmas present."

Bristol didn't recognize the face without its beard, but she knew the voice. "Doberman? Is that you?"

He raised his arm and rattled the silver bracelet.

"How did you get in? Why are you here?"

"The new owner let me in."

"You look different." Bristol saw Kay enter the room. She had on a red party dress. Hector appeared next, not in his work clothes, but dressed in slacks and coat. "What's going on?"

A black Afghan came bounding into the room and jumped up onto Bristol. "Mozart! I thought you were sent to the pound."

"Hector's been taking care of Mozart," said Chase. "Since you adopted me, Bristol. It's my turn. I want to adopt you. That is, if you would be willing to live with us."

"I don't understand."

"I'm the new owner."

"Doberman. You were living on the streets. How?"

"It's a long story."

"Does this mean I get to live here again?"

"That's the idea. Your room is restored, almost as before. Bed, dresser, night stands, even a desk with a bunch of art material, easel, and paper. Have a look. Daleka helped us put everything together. She's moving into the cottage. Hector is coming back too, to manage the property. We're planning to start a woodworking business."

"My son, of course," said Kay, "who you've met, will be living with us too."

Milo walked into the room. "Hi. Again."

Bristol raised her hand in a wave. She smiled, still confused.

"Well," said Chase, "say something."

Bristol remained still. Then she moved toward him, placing her arms around his body with a hug. "I'm sorry, Doberman. For all the mean things I said to you."

"It's okay. I understood why you lashed out. I've experienced my own pain. You made me realize something."

She looked up at him. "What?"

"It's time."

"Time for what?"

"To rise from the ashes. And keep living." He pointed to framed photos arranged along the fireplace mantel. "We owe it to the ones we love and have lost."

Bristol looked at the photo of her father. Another photo showed her as a young child, together with her father, mother, and brother. A photo of Daleka was there too. Also a black-and-white portrait of Kay and Milo. There was even a photo of Hector with his family.

Bristol stared, overwhelmed, processing what all of this meant. Gradually her spunkiness resurfaced and she announced, "Wait here! We're not ready yet. Nobody move!" She ran and disappeared into her bedroom, closing the door behind her.

Chase was as baffled as was everyone else. She emerged after ten minutes holding a sheet of art paper and placed it onto the mantel. Bristol had drawn a man, woman, boy, and girl. A name was beside each figure: Chet. Dayle. Julia. Chase. A rainbow was above them in the sky. At the bottom she had written: Doberman's Family.

"Now we're complete," said Bristol.

Overcome with emotion, Chase said, "You drew a rainbow."

"I felt it needed one."

"Are those music notes inside the arch?"

"Hummingbirds. I can do better. I'll draw a new one."

"No. It's perfect."

Realizing this was her new family, Bristol gave a sprightly laugh, and said, "I can't believe you're going to adopt me, *Doberman!*"

He grinned. Kay was right. His self-sacrifice had saved Bristol, but she had saved him. He looked at the decorated tree with its shiny ornaments and twinkling lights. It didn't matter what month of the year it was. Doberman loved Christmas.

www.ingramcontent.com/pod-product-compliance
Lightning Source LLC
Chambersburg PA
CBHW060509030426
42337CB00015B/1820